The Money Triangle

PHIL BLOWS

COPYRIGHT © 2020

Table of Contents

Foreword vi

Chapter 1 – Money Stories 1

Chapter 2 11
   The Money Triangle 11
   Why Should You Listen to Me? 14

Chapter 3 31
   Who Are We and How Did We Get Here? 31
   What Does the Financial Future Look Like then? ... 38

Chapter 4 43
   Millionaire Mindset 43
      Are You Afraid to Change? 46
      Are You All Talk and No Action? 49
      You Rely on Motivation Instead of Creating a Habit 50
      You Accept Your Excuses 51
      You Give up Before You even Start 53
   The Money Life Balance 58
   Who Wants to Be a Millionaire? 66
      What About the Investment Return that We Are Expecting? 69

How to Spend It 71

You're Spending more than You Think............ 75
Budgeting 77
Keep on Top of Your Regular Bills................ 81
Where Else Can We Save Each Month? 84
    Online Purchases........................... 84
    Eating Out for Lunch 88
    Drinking and Going Out 90
    Smoking 93
    Mobile Phones 94
    Making Impulse Purchases 95
Behavioural Changes............................ 98
    How Do We Combat This?.................... 99
Mismanaging Debt 101
    What Is Good Debt? 105
    What Is a Mortgage? 107
    Credit Rating 110
Summary...................................... 114

How to Earn It 116
The Working World............................ 118
    Timing 122
    Change Your Behaviour 123
Passive Income................................ 125
    Things to Consider When Picking a
    Passive Income Strategy 128
How to Execute Your Side Hustle 131

  MVP 131
 Finding the Right Side Hustle 134
  Step 1: What Are Your Hobbies, Interests, Talents and Skills?................................. 135
  Step 2: Connect the Dots and Look for Trends .. 136
  Step 3: Test the Market 137
  Step 4: Create Social Media and Website Content 138
  Step 5 141
 Passive Income Inspiration..................... 142
  Don't Leave Money on the Table.............. 142
  Teach Your Expertise........................ 146
 Every Day I'm Hustlin' 149
 Side Hustles You Can Start Tomorrow 153
  E-Commerce 154
  Affiliate Marketing 156
  Teespring................................. 157
  The Sharing Economy....................... 157
  Airbnb 157
  DogVacay 158
  Lyft/Uber................................. 158
  UberEats/Deliveroo........................ 159
  Tutoring 160
 Summary..................................... 160

How to Invest It 163

How Investing Drives Wealth Creation 166
Drown Out the Noise 170
    Property 172
    Bonds.................................... 173
    Cash..................................... 174
    Stocks/Equities/Shares 174
    Share Index............................... 174
The Three Rules of Investing 175
    Rule 1: Make Sure You Take on the
    Right Amount of Risk....................... 175
    Rule 2: Don't Try to Beat the Market 181
    Rule 3: Keep an Eye on Fees.................. 184
Summary on Stock Market Investing 187
Property 187
    How to Choose What Type of Property to Buy.. 190
    If You Really Want to be a Property Investor.... 192
    Renting Out Your Property 196
    Beware of the Fine Print 198
    Always Look for Ways to Add Value........... 201
    Overseas Property Investment................. 204
Summary.................................... 207

Your Money Triangle 209
Where Do I Start? 209

Epilogue.. 212
Get Rich or Die Tryin'......................... 212

Acknowledgements 215

About the Author 216

*This book is dedicated to my wife Anna,
without whom none of this would have been possible.*

FOREWORD

Oliver Payne

For a long time I've been a strong believer that managing your money is not rocket science (and even rocket science is still just science!) It fascinates me that so many people drag themselves into work to earn money but don't follow a few simple tricks to turbocharge that money to help put themselves, and their family, in a better place financially. Most people want to stop working at some point in their lives, but then haven't thought about what steps they should take to achieve the financial freedom they need to retire comfortably when they are ready. We are all trying to live our best lives in whatever ways we can: working hard, socialising, eating well, exercising, etc., but it's amazing how many people do not prioritise looking after their finances.

Having read so many poor communications and participated in so many discussions about "engaging" people in how they manage their investments, it doesn't surprise me that people don't know where to start when it comes to improving their finances. The industry is full of jargon, legal caveats and other nonsense that confuses and distracts ordinary people from understanding what they have and what to do. The industry jargon, natural human behaviours and lack of trust in financial services mean most people bury their heads and assume you need to win the lottery or be a .com millionaire in order to become truly wealthy. In practice, there is nothing that complicated about personal finances and financial freedom shouldn't be something that only a privileged few can aspire to. Phil is better than anyone I know at humanising financial well-being by telling stories in an engaging and inspiring way and using the Money Triangle as a concept that sits behind a series of simple solutions that everyone can understand and benefit from to improve their financial well-being and set out a path to financial freedom.

By painting a picture of the human side of finances, this book cuts through the jargon, the nonsense and the excuses and inspires everyone to get on and make changes (both big and small) to improve their lives and work towards financial freedom. The three sides of the Money Triangle are brought to life in an engaging and inspiring way without confusing jargon or patronising the reader. There are few people who wouldn't benefit from reading this book and taking some or all of the actions to help achieve financial freedom.

I clearly remember, at an early age, the attraction of being able to "live off the interest" of your savings. It seemed to me like all your problems would be solved if you could sit back and watch the interest roll in, but, as a young boy, I thought this was just for Formula 1 drivers and lottery winners. As a grown up, I now realise we are all hoping to one day have enough savings to be able to stop working and live off the interest. All we need to do is set out our path to financial freedom and make a few sensible decisions to improve how we earn, spend and save our money.

Although there is no rocket science behind the Money Triangle, there is the miracle of compound interest ("the 8th wonder of the world" – according to Einstein) which can turbocharge small tweaks to your money to make a big difference. I'm very excited to think of all the changes people will make to their finances, after reading this book and the cumulative effect of compound interest helping savings work harder to create extra wealth and empower many people to achieve their financial freedom.

Following the simple approaches set out in this book to increase your earnings, reduce spending and improve investments will help create a solid foundation for anyone to build towards their own personal financial freedom. Once achieved, this can take away the pressure and stress of money worries and open a world of possibilities to prioritise what really matters for you.

It all starts with small changes that anyone can make, and it hopefully it ends with a new world of possibilities when you have reached financial freedom.

Oliver Payne – European Pensions Manager and Actuary, Ford Motor Company Ltd

Chapter 1 – Money Stories

They say money doesn't bring happiness,
but everyone still wants to prove it for themselves.
– Anonymous

Michael was not born with a silver spoon in his mouth. His mother worked in a canning factory, and his father was an RAF engineer. When Michael was just a toddler, his father was jailed in a military prison for 11 years for stabbing a couple on a night out. The incident happened after an altercation at a local dance that he had attended. His parents separated when he was just 7 years old, and his father passed away soon after from a heart attack. To say Michael's early years were not easy would be an understatement.

After the death of his father, Michael's mother went on to marry several men, one of whom would beat him and then lock him in his room for hours. Whether due to his chaotic upbringing or just due to being dealt a lousy hand in the genetic lottery, Michael also suffered severely from dyslexia and had ADHD, so by the time he left secondary school he was barely literate.

Following in his father's footsteps, Michael received a custodial sentence for shoplifting at the age of 13 and was sent to the Hollesley Bay Prison in Suffolk, England. One good thing that happened during his incarceration, and which was a credit to the youth prison system, was that he finally learnt to read and write.

After his initial stay in prison, Michael mostly kept out of trouble, and once old enough to work, he managed to get a job working for the local council as a bin man. Picking up people's litter would, in ordinary cases, have been the last time that we might have heard about Michael from Suffolk had it not been for a fateful trip to his local corner shop.

It was on this visit that the then 19-year-old Michael, who was wearing an electronic tag from a recent run-in with the police to monitor his movements, did something that would propel him towards becoming a household name in the UK. He bought a lottery ticket for the first time.

As luck would have it, on the following Saturday, Michael's numbers, which had been randomly selected at the time of purchase, came up and he won £9.7 million. Michael had no bank account at the time of his win and was even turned down when trying to set one up afterwards, due to his criminal record.

What followed was an epic spending and partying spree on booze, drugs and hookers, which saw him banned from driving for six months having been caught at the wheel of his new £49,000 BMW without L-plates and insurance in 2004.

In June 2005, Michael was summoned to court after it was found that whilst drunk he had been seen catapulting steel balls from his Mercedes van which resulted in breaking 32 car and shop windows. He was sentenced to 240 hours of community service.

In February 2006, he was jailed for nine months for affray. It was noted in court whilst being sentenced that, since 1997, Michael had 42 previous offences on record.

Where is he now?

In May 2010, Michael, also referred in the press as 'the lotto lout', applied for his old job as a bin man and eventually ended up working in a slaughter house where, having spent the entirety of his winnings, he earns £400 a week and rents a modest flat, a far cry from the English mansion in which he once lived. When asked how he feels about the whole experience, Michael insists he has no regrets.

Mark was born on May 14, 1984, in White Plains, New York. Mark had a comfortable upper-middle-class upbringing with a loving family life where he was given access to private tutors and encouraged to explore his many flourishing talents, whether this be fencing at school or a natural proclivity towards programming computer games.

Mark was raised in the village of Dobbs Ferry by his father, Edward, who ran a dental practice attached to the family's home. His mother, Karen, was a psychiatrist by training but gave this up to focus on family life after Mark's three siblings were born.

As Mark grew older, his interest in computers began to flourish, and he was recognised as a prodigy from a young age. Mark had several artistic friends, who would often visit his house and get him to convert their work into computer games that they would then enjoy together.

Mark started using computers to solve everyday problems when he built a messaging program so that his father's receptionist could inform him of a patient arriving without shouting across the room. The messaging app also meant his father could talk to the family in the house from their attached dentist surgery. He used Atari BASIC to create this program at the age of 13 but quickly lost interest in this project when Skype and similar messaging apps appeared soon afterwards.

Mark got his first taste of success in 2000 when in high school he used machine learning to determine a user's music preferences and then recommended more music based on what they liked. Despite this being a universal service today, when Mark built it in 2000, it was highly innovative, and he received offers from both Microsoft and AOL who wanted to buy his software, called Synapse, and offer him a job. In a surprising move that would set Mark up for future success, he decided not to sell and instead posted the app online for free and enrolled at Harvard University.

Where is Mark today?

Well, as you might have guessed, Mark is indeed Mark Zuckerberg, the founder of Facebook who at the end of 2019, 19 years after turning down a rumoured $1 million for Synapse, is now worth $74 billion.

In 2000, Lidia had just graduated with a Marketing degree at the age of 25. Fresh from college she had ambition and was desperate to get her career and finances moving in the right direction having taken on large amounts of student debt to finance her time at university.

Her timing couldn't have been worse. With the bursting of the dot com bubble and subsequent global recession, the job market completely dried up, and Lidia found herself in the unemployed queue along with many other recent graduates.

Lidia, who was living in San Francisco, knew she wouldn't last long in the area with no job due to the high cost of living. Frustratingly the only area of the job market that was hiring seemed to be retail. Lidia, keen to get started somewhere, got a full-time job at Williams-Sonoma earning $9.25 an hour. Crucially, on top of this salary, which was only slightly higher than minimum wage, the company offered to match a proportion of any money that an employee paid into their long-term savings plan.

Lidia's boyfriend at the time worked for a financial services firm and, being familiar with the importance of retirement savings, encouraged Lidia to start investing as much as she could afford into a highly tax efficient long-term savings account.

The problem was that when she looked at her earnings and lifestyle, Lidia felt she couldn't afford to contribute anything towards her savings. Even if she did, she asked herself, would she live long enough to spend her money in retirement? However, the more Lidia learnt, the more her attitude towards saving shifted. She realised that she was not only saving money for herself but for her future family. She also realised that much of the spending she was doing, if she was brutally honest, was on luxuries that she didn't need.

So, despite earning very little, Lidia sacrificed spending money on luxuries and aimed to contribute 15% of her salary into her savings account. Living on so little wasn't easy. Her rent alone cost $700 after which she could barely afford to enjoy any of the lively city that was on her doorstep.

Lidia's savings rate ended up averaging 12% of her income or around $2,400 in the first year. However, her employer topped this amount up as part of an employee savings program. This meant in her first year she had saved $3,600 whilst earning just $20,000 per year.

Not only did Lidia manage to save $3,600, but she used her low-wage job as a stepping stone to better opportunities and higher incomes. After just a year of working for $9.25 an hour, Lidia was promoted within Williams-Sonoma to a corporate position that doubled her annual salary. Whilst she continued to work hard and earn salary increases over the years, it all started with her near-minimum-wage retail job.

Where is she today?

Now, 15 years since she started her low-wage job, Lidia Shong's regular savings habit and wage growth mean she has saved up an impressive $400,000. Lidia has combined a dedicated savings habit with a hard-working attitude to climb the corporate ladder and get on the road to financial freedom.

Lidia is quick to point out that even if she'd never achieved any salary increases and had merely continued to save 12% , alongside the employer match with her original $20,000 annual income, she estimates that she would have over $100,000 worth of retirement savings today. By the age of 65, she would have saved $937,000 — close to a million dollars.

Motivated by her own journey, Lidia joined a company that provides people with free financial planning support and she is working hard to help others that are in the same position she was in.

These three stories from very different people highlight just how varied our relationship with money can be. What sparked Lidia's obsession with saving? What led to Michael's downfall when given a lottery win? Why did Mark not take a million dollars at a young age?

The way we manage our money and the wealth we create or retain is fundamentally influenced by our early life and the lessons we learn from those around us. In the previous stories, we see three different reactions to people who came into money, some healthy some incredibly damaging (both to themselves and those around them). Money need not be the route of all evil and once understood should be used as a tool to help us achieve what we want out of life.

Given that the chances of the average reader winning the lottery are somewhere in the region of 1 in 45 million, I will not be devoting this book to Michael and strategies around picking winning numbers.

According to an article in Fast Company, '*Why Most Venture-Backed Companies Fail*,' in 2017, just 56 companies achieved the milestone of being valued at over $1 billion despite over 600,000 companies being founded in the UK alone – better odds than the lottery but I am not going to say that reading this book alone is going to make you the next Zuckerberg leading you to start a billion-dollar company. This book will, however, get you on track to adding useful additional sources of income to help you achieve your financial goals.

This book is aimed at the Lidias of the world. Many of us with a just a few tweaks and early sacrifices can, just as Lidia proved, get on the road to financial freedom. I hope that by working together, using the simple concept of the Money Triangle, we can help you get on track to building real, lasting wealth, regardless of your background or current habits towards money.

The subjects we tackle are those many people would rather not talk about. Money has long been viewed as a taboo subject, as it is perceived as impolite or arrogant to do so. For this reason, many of our financial problems fester and cause lasting damage in the form of poor credit ratings or financially induced stress and anxiety.

This book is for the average person in the street who wants to improve their spending habits, earn more and invest it successfully. Perhaps this is the first finance book you have picked up. Maybe it is the 100th; either way, by the end of this book, you will have a plan as to what you need to do to create an exciting financial future.

By the end of this book, I want you to not only feel able to manage your finances but be confident that, through careful planning and some sacrifice, building a net worth of more than £1 million over your lifetime is absolutely attainable. Why £1 million? In short, this is the minimum amount needed to achieve financial freedom. £1 million can generate a perpetual income of roughly £35,000 per year so it represents the minimum amount of money that you will need to live comfortably once you decide to give up work forever.

I warn you now; this is not a get rich quick book. This book will not make you a millionaire in two years, although it contains examples of people who did. I will leave those claims to other books. The purpose of this book is a reality check, an insurance policy if you will.

Many of us dream, albeit with no plan how, that all our financial issues will be solved once we win the lottery, start that successful company or get promoted to CEO. However, let us consider for a moment that if none of these things do pan out for you (as indeed they don't for the vast majority of people), what will you do to make sure you don't spend your later years in poverty?

This book is here to ensure that even if your career plans and dreams don't come true as you hope, at least you will not be financially destitute; indeed it will not matter as you have planned accordingly and built a pot of money that will give you the lifestyle that you want.

To help you achieve your goals, I have drawn upon the combined experience of some of the most successful people in the world of finance, technology, entrepreneurship and lifestyle design. Their stories not only inspire us but, when studied, reveal certain common traits that have been core to their success. Adopting these is key to following in their footsteps.

The other purpose of this book is to get you to a place where you no longer feel stressed about money. According to a new Chartered Institute of Personnel and Development report in the UK on the topic of financial well-being, one in four employees felt their workplace performance was being affected by financial worries. I want to take away this stress so you can focus on your career or starting a business. Let's clear away the fear and doubt so you can begin hitting your big, hairy, audacious goals.

For many, this book will require a mindset change. I ask you to bear with me as achieving the goal of financial freedom is a marathon and not a sprint. I will at times ask you to carry out specific exercises in this book. I encourage you to follow them as it is only by applying the lessons in the book to your circumstances that you will begin to understand the power of these strategies. Just reading this book is not enough.

If we look closely at Lidia's story, we can see that a simple mindset change led to a complete change in her financial future. When she started, she couldn't see the benefit of saving money for the long term. It was only after nudging from her partner and a few years of seeing savings build up that she committed to it. She is not alone, and I am always amazed by the good and bad decisions that we see people make with their finances every day and how, by just tweaking a few small things, we can fundamentally change your financial future.

Chapter 2

"The art is not in making money, but in keeping it."
– Proverb

The Money Triangle

The Money Triangle is a simple concept that can act as a foundation to help anyone build wealth and eventually financial freedom. There are three sides that make up the Money Triangle:

1. How to spend it
2. How to earn it
3. How to invest it

Triangles are the strongest shape in nature because any added force is evenly spread between each of the three sides. The Money Triangle is no different; if you balance all three sides, you will have a strong foundation to build up wealth. However, without having all three sides balanced, it is rarely easy to achieve any sort of long-term wealth.

Put simply:

- It doesn't matter how much you earn if you immediately spend everything.
- You won't be able to invest enough if you don't have enough earnings.

- If you invest your money poorly, it won't grow into anything meaningful.

You can play around with each combination but only by spending wisely, earning more than enough to cover your essential living costs and then investing it wisely will you have a strong Money Triangle and a foundation to build up to financial freedom.

The next couple of chapters give some much-needed context to both the problem we are looking to solve and the mindset needed to do it. I will then break down the Money Triangle into its constituent parts of spending, earning and investing and show you how to achieve balance and rigidity in each one.

It may seem odd to carry out these steps in this order, i.e. looking at 'How to Spend It' first; however, money often magnifies existing habits, so if these are unhealthy, such as spending more than you earn, you can expect having more money will lead to more of the same. For this reason, the first section is aimed at growing healthy and considered spending habits to give a strong platform from which we will build our wealth.

We then move on to the next constituent of the Money Triangle: 'How to Earn It'. Developing multiple income streams from profitable side hustles or passive income strategies can be the quickest way to become wealthy. This section looks at case studies and lessons learnt from those who have built significant wealth via this channel.

Our final section is 'How to Invest It'. Choosing what to do with any leftover money can be extremely stressful. The world of finance can be confusing. What we want to do in this section is to provide simple strategies to make sure your money is working hard for you so that you can focus on the other two sides of the Money Triangle. We will also show in this section how many of the finance 'professionals' out there may not be worth listening to.

Financial freedom is a term that gets used a lot. What then is it? Cicero defined freedom as 'the power to live as one wishes', and I feel this sums it up nicely. Financial freedom is simply the ability to meet your financial needs whilst living as you please. For many this might mean having the ability to never need to work as you are able to live off the passive interest generated by your investments. For others, this might mean being able to work in a flexible manner taking regular career breaks as and when you choose.

The point is financial freedom is unique to each person and defining what it looks like for you is a key first step towards creating a plan that achieves it.

I felt compelled to write this book despite hundreds of books already out there that cover elements of this topic. I find many of these books will only focus on one element of the Money Triangle and as such can leave gaps in the behaviours people go on to adopt. For example, you can be the world's greatest investor, but without the money to invest in the first place, these strategies are useless.

On a similar note, the Financial Independence Retire Early (FIRE) movement has seen people turn to extremely frugal lifestyles which, although fantastic for getting them to retire early, will do little to allow them to live a meaningful life before then. The Money Triangle provides balance whereby we reduce our spending to acceptable levels but also use additional income streams and investing strategies to achieve financial freedom without the same level of personal sacrifice needed.

I hope you enjoy this book and it inspires you to get out there and make positive changes in your life. I hope to one day include your story in future iterations of this book and detail exactly how you got on the path to financial freedom.

Why Should You Listen to Me?

Over the past 4 years, I have spoken with over 500 companies about the challenges their employees face with their finances. I have used this feedback, along with 15 years of experience in finance, to help develop a methodology to help people better manage their money and get on track for the kind of financial outcome about which they can get excited.

Through my work with employers, I have been lucky enough to obtain insight into the daily financial habits of people from all walks of life. This has involved analysing the finances of employees of some of the UK's best known businesses including large retailers, charities, as well as government employees and those working for the NHS.

In 2018 alone, through work with my employer, Wealth Wizards, we helped over 10,000 people gain insight into their financial priorities, get hold of their finances and take action towards improving their financial future.

When I speak with HR teams about what they currently do to help their employees with their finances, I sometimes encounter amazing teams who are tackling these problems successfully and really care about the future livelihood of their people. However, overall, the most common response is to point to a reward program that gives them incentives such as money off technology purchases and two for one cinema tickets and meal deals. If anything, these programs are encouraging people to spend, not save, and are exacerbating the problems we see in how people manage their money.

This lack of strategy can be frustrating when the link between employee performance and financial stress is so clear. We partnered with the Centre for Economics and Business Research to look at the attitudes of employers and employees at 500 leading companies in the UK. The results were shocking.

Of the companies that we spoke to, three out of five employers would prefer an employee work for them indefinitely rather than retire at 65. Only 25% of them offered employees some advice or education around their finances and employers are more likely to hire someone older with more experience despite acknowledging that this will mean fewer opportunities for young people entering the workforce.

What about the people working at these companies? Do they share their company's desire to work for their employers indefinitely? The average age that the people we spoke to would like to scale back their work or retire was 60. We followed this up with a question around when people thought they would be financially able to retire, and most people said 69. Depressingly, one in five people said they are expecting to work until the day they die!

Let's take an example; the average person in the UK, according to ONS data, is earning £30,420 per year or

£22,241 after tax. They can expect to have a pot of money at the point of retirement that when combined with the state Pension will give them an income of around £11,000 a year. I don't think anyone would aspire to a retirement that gives them that sort of lifestyle; however, most of us are sleepwalking into this sort of outcome.

Against this depressing backdrop of never being able to retire and working for companies who aren't concerned about what age we stop working, something must be done. We need the knowledge and tools to solve the problem ourselves as we are highly unlikely to get help from anywhere else.

If, due to a rapidly ageing workforce, opportunities for the current generation are likely to decrease, that means we must do more to make ourselves independent and self-sufficient when it comes to our finances. As job security decreases, we also need to develop multiple sources of income to protect us from a job market that is highly likely to change due to the emergence of artificial intelligence that will automate many current jobs but also open the door for new opportunities.

In many cases, we can't rely on employers to give us a job for life or parents to provide us with large sums of money to support us. We must ensure that we capitalise on opportunities to make money, spend it wisely and, when we can, invest it efficiently. By doing this, we will increase our financial resilience and independence.

I have loved finance, investing and innovative ways of making money for as long as I can remember. When I was eight and discovered that we received a free local newspaper through the door every week, I would spend my evening combing through the job section looking at which paid the most money and if any of them would employ an eight-year-old!

Growing up I was fortunate to have a comfortable childhood where we were not struggling for money. However, an early experience did bring money into focus from an early age. When I was 10 years old, I had the opportunity to move from the private school I was attending to a local grammar school. In order to do so, I would need to pass entry exams and score well enough to be accepted. Fortunately, I passed and was offered a place. I felt proud about the move as, even at a young age, it was obvious that private school fees were having a big impact on our wider family finances and it was a great opportunity to give my parents some breathing room.

All started well after a period of adjustment and settling in; however, very quickly I found that with school days often finishing at 2:30 pm, I was bored and had little to do in the afternoons. Things started to spiral as I fell out with friends and I often found myself finding excuses not to go to school which had a big impact on my studying. After 2 years the situation was becoming desperate and having hidden things from my parents, I spoke with them. I will be forever grateful that they responded decisively and at big personal cost they moved me to a local private school. From this moment I never looked back and count them as some of the best years of my life.

This stressful situation in a formative period of my life shaped my view of money and I think is part of the reason that I was so motivated to learn everything I could about it and gain financial freedom as soon as I could.

Despite my early exuberance trawling through job adverts, it wasn't until I had completed my final exams at university that I decided to start looking into what I wanted to do when I entered the world of work. All I knew at the time was that I needed a job that paid well and quickly as my parents were living abroad and I didn't have the option to move back in with them again.

After a brief google search, I stumbled across the efinancialcareers.com website that was full of jobs for graduates looking to make their mark on the world of finance. Having been a keen reader of any financial literature, I could get my hands on throughout university, from Michael Lewis' 'Liars Poker' to Benjamin Graham's financial tome, 'Security Analysis'. I thought finance was the career path for me, despite my degree being in Geological Sciences. Fortunately, this was 2005, and the financial job market was robust which meant I quickly received a job offer for a foreign exchange company within their sales team.

The job was fairly straightforward; after an initial crash course in how currency markets worked from Micky, a 50-year veteran of the financial markets, I was on the phone. My job was to call retail investors and convince them why the company I worked for would give them a better rate of exchange for any overseas property purchases or investments than their high street bank. This was a reasonably easy sell at the time as high street banks were (and still are) charging upwards of 1% for currency transactions and I was able to offer them 0.5%. On a £100,000 overseas transaction, this was a saving of £500 so effectively free money, albeit after completing a little paperwork.

This job provided a fascinating insight into the motivations of why people invest in certain assets and meant that

I spent a lot of time talking with people who were looking at retiring. What was interesting was either through luck, or careful planning, many of the clients I spoke to were realising their lifetime dreams of selling up in the UK and retiring to sunny locations around the world. I made a point of getting to know the clients who were making the large transactions to see how they had made their money. These clients were just as likely to be entrepreneurs as they were salaried employees or successful property investors, and there didn't seem to be any secret regarding their day-to-day profession. However, one thing they all had in common was that they had started investing either in themselves or financial markets from an early age.

Throughout my time at this job, I dived headlong into learning everything I could about personal finance and how to make money from investing, and this meant reading every book I could get my hands on. I wanted to broaden my product knowledge from the currency markets where I worked, to cover everything from stocks and bonds to complex derivatives. That meant reading biographies from some of the best performing fund managers in the world, 'how-to' books for the novice investor and publications focused on the psychology of investing and how to counteract many of the human biases we have that lead to poor investment performance.

It was though this crash course in finance that I realised, although fun, my work in the Foreign Exchange markets was only a small fraction of what I needed to learn and I was limiting myself to just one aspect of a vast and complex world of financial instruments, and I needed a more holistic real-world education. After only nine months in the job, I moved to a trading desk at a boutique investment house in the heart of the financial district of London.

Changing jobs is never easy and plucking up the courage to leave an employer who has treated you well can be daunting. For me, when making the decision of when to leave, I drew up a list of pros and cons for each opportunity. It was clear that my career path and future earnings were limited where I was, and I had little to lose trying something new given how young I was.

My new role was my first experience within a regulated financial business and required me to take three exams. Some of these were interesting and needed further learning around stocks and derivatives markets, and others were a little dull and meant I had to learn regulatory laws verbatim. I was keen to hit the ground running in my new role, so I worked morning and night during my gardening leave and completed the exams in an intense three-week period instead of the usual 6 months.

'George' was one of our clients. A successful hedge fund manager by day, he managed billions for institutional investors in low-risk bond portfolios. However, George lodged £100,000 in an account with us. He then used our trading platform to jump around investments in foreign exchange, leveraged stocks and futures contracts. When I questioned him as to why such an experienced investor was throwing money around on wild punts, he simply told me this was a slush fund of money that he liked to have fun with and didn't really care what the outcome was.

A few weeks and hundreds of trades later, George had grown his account to over £1 million and had exposure of several million pounds in a variety of assets. This huge run in good fortune would have had me trying to cash in my chips, but not George. Another two weeks and hundreds of trades later, the account stood at zero. George, totally unfazed by the reversal in fortune, simply laughed and funded another £100,000 to get started again. This was merely a hobby for him, albeit a very expensive one!

I thoroughly enjoyed the job but for the first six months only earned my basic salary of £18,000 which had to cover the cost of a flat in London, student loan repayments and the occasional night out. This meant at the end of every month I was often completely maxed out on my overdraft and credit card and would have the bank on the phone asking when I was likely to reduce the balances that I was running. Often even after payday, I would still be sitting in my overdraft paying somewhere in the region of 20% interest for the money that I had borrowed from the bank.

After 3 months of this back and forward and the stress of the monthly calls from the bank, I'd had enough. I forced myself to write a strict budget that would put me in a better position. This meant cutting all my expenses other than rent and bills by at least 50%. I stopped going out, and when I did, I made sure I didn't buy expensive drinks. I purchased cheaper meals and tried to plan more to reduce wastage. I downgraded to the most affordable mobile phone package and had an old phone. At the same time, I automated my savings by transferring money immediately into a savings account the day I received it on payday. After only 2 months of this frugal living, I was sitting in positive territory at the end of each month and building my financial resilience. Better yet, I wasn't receiving the monthly phone calls from the bank which lifted a serious weight off my mind.

Alongside this new appreciation of budgeting, I was quickly finding I was in my element on the trading desk. I quickly became the highest-performing adviser bringing on and retaining more clients than the rest of the combined sales team – something I attributed to being first in the office and last to leave. Within 6 months I was named Sales Director which meant I took a cut of the revenues of the whole trading desk. A few months after becoming Sales Director, my boss took me out to lunch to drop a bombshell. He was moving with his fiancée back to her hometown in Tulsa in Oklahoma, and I was being promoted to run the desk.

With that, I was charged by the company to run the trading desk at the age of 22 managing a team of 15 traders and advisers who oversaw millions in client assets. What I didn't know at the time was things were about to get extremely tough.

Six months after taking over the business, we were growing at a fantastic rate and markets were booming. One sunny Monday I got off the tube at Cannon Street and entered the office as usual at 7:15 am to set up for the trading day ahead. Instead of being met by the usual quiet office and beautiful views over the City of London, there was a team of administrators from an accountancy firm blocking access to the office.

Unfortunately, the business of which we were an appointed representative and who provided us with our regulatory umbrella, was not doing so well. Several brokers who worked for the parent company had been selling stock in what I later found out were called regulation S securities. 'Reg S' stocks were US-based companies where investors, having purchased a stake in the business, were unable to sell it for at least a few years by which time the corporation was typically insolvent and the shares worthless. As you would expect, many of these investors were extremely upset, and there were multiple court cases against the parent company. Think Wolf of Wall Street and you wouldn't be far off.

I was not aware of any of this when I arrived at the office on that fateful Monday. The administrators informed me that they were the new owners of the business. The whole company was liquidated, and my team was fired on the spot. To rub salt into the wound, it was the day before payday, and we were told to get in line to claim any lost earnings a process that took several months and gave us pennies on the pound.

This event occurred at the worst possible time. With my earnings increasing rapidly, I had just bought my first property and taken out an expensive mortgage. The flat needed serious work, and I had no money or income to pay for it. I had entered one of the most stressful periods of my financial life at a time when I was desperately trying to keep together my old team and client base and move whatever we had left after the administrators had torn it to pieces to another company.

Financial stress is never pleasant, and with all that was going on, I struggled to sleep and concentrate on solving the problems I was facing. It seemed at times that even simple tasks like moving furniture into the new flat would cause bouts of intense anxiety. The best way I found to overcome this feeling was to throw myself into finding a new home for the business. I treated it like a job, getting up early, putting on a suit and going into the city and doing a full working day of researching new employment opportunities whilst drinking tap water in local coffee shops. This had the added advantage of any opportunity I uncovered I could be there at a moment's notice, and after a short period of time, I started getting traction with a few opportunities.

To make ends meet, I was able to get a few friends from university to move into the flat despite it being in poor condition. This additional source of income was invaluable during those lean months and meant I didn't need to sell the flat. Over time it has also become a significant long-term investment, doubling in price whilst retaining a rental yield of 5%.

Luckily, through an old contact, I was able to move the business to a new home within 3 months. As chance would have it, it was my former employer who had decided to expand into a more extensive array of markets other than foreign exchange, precisely the reason I had left!

With the backing of a more significant business behind us, we quickly built the private client investment business with many of our old clients joining us at our new operation. I was also able to expand the services we offered to clients and gave them access to a new managed account service where clients could invest money which I traded on their behalf.

The primary strategy that I was using to invest client money was to look at two very similar companies, for example, British American Tobacco and Imperial Tobacco, and then buy one and sell the other. What I was betting on was that one would outperform the other so it could make money regardless of which direction the market was going in. In the case of these tobacco stocks, both companies were of a similar size, in the same industry and within the same index in the stock market. The price difference between the two would often move sharply as there was news on one stock or the other and I would bet that this would correct back to the mean. As volatility in financial markets began to pick up in late 2008 and 2009, this was a hugely profitable strategy.

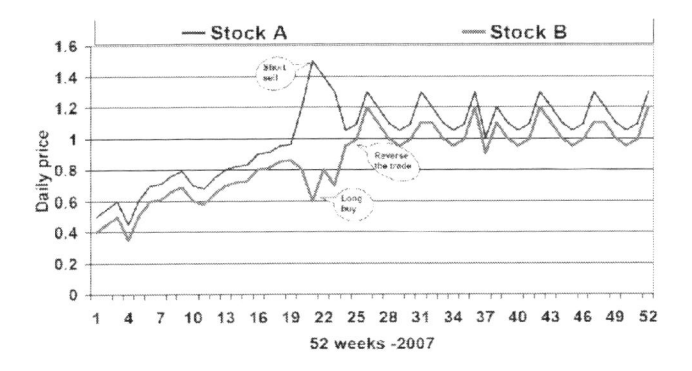

Our business was growing well, and our advice and managed account service profited even through the wild swings and enormous pressure and stress of the 2008 financial crisis. With the business thriving, I was able to invest my own money in the strategies that we were using and realise returns in the high double digits.

Despite the success our business was having, the financial crisis was battering traditional financial institutions and consequently some of the poorest members of society. The bursting of the US housing market bubble saw millions of people, usually those from the most deprived areas already, lose their homes.

It was also at this point that some of our parent company's more substantial shareholders, who had been decimated by the financial crisis and involved in much of the selling of high-risk mortgage derivatives, decided they wanted to scale back the risk in all of their operations regardless of recent performance. They decided to close our profitable managed account service and lay off half my team.

I found this incredibly demotivating and having lived and worked in London for six years decided it was time for a change. This was not an easy decision to make as I would be giving up everything I had built up over my career and would have to start from scratch. However, once again, when looking at the pros and cons of the situation there was very little downside. I always had the confidence that I could find a sales job that would make ends meet if I didn't like my career move, so why not roll the dice?

Through a contact I had in a previous job, I interviewed for a role based in a village near Geneva called Nyon. This could not have been more different to city life; however, it provided exactly the change I was looking for.

Luckily, I was successful and in 2010 moved out to work for a derivate business that advised global investment banks on their foreign exchange strategies.

Switzerland provided a huge culture shock, not only was I living in a sleepy village on the shores of Lake Geneva surrounded by vineyards, the work was incredibly fast-paced, and much of the trading now took place via an open outcry system where brokers on the desk would shout orders at each other. The environment was harsh but exciting, and you needed the ability to think quickly on your feet.

In my first year at the business, we were swamped as we dealt with banks transferring money in and out of Russia. Russia decided at this point it was a good idea to invade Ukraine, and as a result, every investment bank decided to move their money out of the Russian ruble and move it back into dollars fearing impending sanctions. This led to considerable increases in the daily number of transactions we were completing.

It was during this explosive event with client orders that needed to be filled and the volume of the desk at a fever pitch that I found myself in need of a calculator. I had been given a big client order and had no idea how much of it I still had left to buy. I noticed that a Swiss colleague of mine, Beat, had stolen my calculator, so I started shouting at him to give it back; however, he was equally busy trying to fill his own client's orders. After a heated 30 seconds or so, I started to look elsewhere and missed Beat in frustration launch the calculator directly at me and subsequently bounce straight off my head. Already uptight and under pressure, this almost descended into a full-blown fistfight; however, the need to continue filling orders took priority. This adrenalin-fuelled environment once again highlighted how easy it is for financial markets to lose perspective and pure panic to take over. It is these behaviours that so often lead to investors losing money as they sell investments at the worst possible time. To make money from the markets, cool heads must prevail.

With my finances now in a better position, I was able to look at investing money for the long-term and plan for retirement. Although having knowledge of the financial markets, I was a complete novice when investing for myself in complicated tax structures in Switzerland. I therefore asked around my friends for some help. Sadly, this led to me getting scammed by a financial adviser.

The adviser in question was a friend and someone I knew very well in the small, close-knit community of Nyon. He worked for 'the largest independent financial adviser in the world' and sold me a regular investment scheme. The scheme involved putting a fixed sum into an account each month which was invested in funds on my behalf, and over a period of years, I would receive certain tax benefits as part of the investment.

I contributed to this account as I was looking to build up some money to buy a flat and needed somewhere better than the bank to let my money grow. The problems appeared when the time came to take my money out. What my adviser had failed to tell me was that the first 2 years of contributions which amounted to about £15,000 were purely there to cover his fees and I could only take out balances above this figure. The key lesson here is read the small print and if you don't understand something then ask! You should not invest in something that is so complicated you don't understand it, so if this is the case, run a mile!

By this point, my adviser had left the country and moved on to Australia, so I wasn't getting any help from him. The Swiss regulator was even less help and claimed the firm didn't need to be regulated in Switzerland despite what they were doing so wouldn't intervene. They suggested I take legal advice which, in Switzerland, would have cost me more than what I was trying to claim back.

This is one of those harsh lessons that we learn and one of the reasons advisers have such a bad name despite there being some incredibly talented and honest ones. In retrospect, I trusted too much in someone, so didn't read the small print carefully enough and should have known better.

Switzerland was a fantastic experience; however, after 6 years, having survived multiple emerging market crises and studying at a local University to get an MBA under my belt, I decided it was time to move back with my fiancée to the UK.

During my time in Switzerland, I had applied to a number of roles back in the UK, but it was through my existing network that I was able to find a suitable opportunity, this time with a tech start-up with a simple mission in mind: help 1 million people feel more in control of their finances by 2020. Having experienced both the good, the bad and the ugly in this area, I thought it was an ideal place to join.

In this book, it is not only the lessons I have learnt that I want to share but also draw upon the experiences of everyday people who have amazing stories of how they climbed out of debt to achieve financial freedom. I also want to share many of the tips from highly experienced entrepreneurs who have created multiple income streams, investment gurus who have built vast wealth through careful investment selection and lifestyle experts who can help get us into the right mindset.

Many people in society are extremely disengaged in their finances, and this is going to have a huge impact on the happiness and stress people will experience later in life. I hope together we can use the concept of the Money Triangle to help you avoid this outcome and make you one of the fortunate people who gets money to work as a tool to help you achieve your goals as opposed to a source of worry. Perhaps you will even share that knowledge to help others.

Chapter 3

"Money is only a tool. It will take you wherever you wish, but it will not replace you as the driver."
– Ayn Rand

Who Are We and How Did We Get Here?

"Maybe every generation thinks the next one is the end of it all. Bet there are people in the Bible walking around, complaining about kids today." – Roger Sterling Mad Men

Before diving into the detail of how to build your Money Triangle, it's worth spending some time reflecting on exactly who you are. The modern-day workforce consists of five generations all exhibiting very different attitudes to their finances. These include:

- The Silents, characterised by their hard work ethic and attitude towards saving, were born between 1925 and 1946.

- Baby boomers, many of whom came into their heyday in the booming 1980s, were born between 1946 and 1964.

- Generation X, born between 1964 and 1981, are often described as leaning towards a balanced life.

- Millennials or Generation Y: you may not want to admit it, but if you were born between the early 1980s to about the mid-1990s, you are indeed classified as a millennial. The reason for this title is that they are the first graduating class of 2000 – the new millennium who are entering the workforce.

- Generation Z are all those born after 1995 who are usually stereotyped as being tech-savvy and entrepreneurial.

Although many commentators will often class people based on the era in which they were born, it is fair to say that each generation is so diverse that it is pointless to try and stereotype. Whether it is a retiree getting on the housing ladder for the first time or a millennial selling their first business and looking for investments, when trying to help people, we must focus on the individual.

It is therefore fair to say we have an incredibly diverse population facing a variety of financial issues all having very different experiences and influences when it comes to how they view their finances.

A good place to start perhaps is with the largest cohort currently in the workforce. According to the Institute of Leadership and Management, 50% of today's workforce will fall into the Millennial or Gen Z category, so it is worth studying what sort of environment this cohort has grown up in.

This generation entered the world of work anywhere between 2001 and 2015. This means they either hit their stride just as the financial crisis kicked off or joined it when the after-effects were still being felt, and businesses were cutting back their workforce whilst desperately trying not to be disrupted by the latest tech start-up. Either way, it's fair to say it has probably not been a walk in the park compared with older peers.

"When previous generations went into jobs, either as young people without a degree or as graduates, the expectation would have been fairly rapid salary progression over the first three or four years, perhaps as much as 10 per cent a year," says Stewart Robertson, senior economist for the UK and Europe at Aviva Investors.

Hmmm… I hear many a millennial think that doesn't sound anything like the reality I experienced. And they would be right. Stewart goes on to say, *"that wasn't the case for those who entered the labour market post-crisis, who experienced quite fierce austerity. The squeeze from 2009 to 2014 was probably the worst in the post-war period."*

Credit: Banksy

According to research by the Resolution Foundation, Millennials in the UK stand to earn £12,500 less during their 20s than their counterparts in Generation X, and increasingly, we see millennials use their expensive flashy degrees to fill part-time and low-skilled roles. The effect on wages has been even more pronounced in the USA, where the Journal of Labour market statistics suggests a typical student who graduated in 2009 stood to earn $58,600 less over the following decade than an average graduate in 2007 which is a decent house deposit.

Effectively, those millennials entering the workforce have entered a world of work which is not as comfortable as that faced by the baby boomer generation, jobs are no longer for life, and they no longer have access to a gold-plated final salary pension scheme. Getting on the housing ladder has proved tough with houses now costing ten times the average starting salary.

Millennials also have less wealth than previous generations with 18- to 34-year-olds having a net worth of just £8,000 compared with £14,000 for those of the same age in 1995. Millennials, keen to be educated, have been exploited with inflation-busting increases in tuition fees which have climbed 243% since 1995, at a time when wage growth has remained stagnant, leading to enormous debt within this cohort. For example, the baby boomer generation (those born soon after the end of WW2) on average had to work for 306 hours at minimum wage to cover the cost of four years at public college, whereas the millennial generation will now need to work for 4,459 hours, according to the National Centre for Education Statistics. These calculations were based on tuition fees for a university course in the USA lasting 4 years from 1973–1976 and 2003–2006.

So, in other words, compared to previous generations, when it comes to money, it sucks if you have recently started out.

The world of finance has become more complicated than ever with constantly changing regulations driven by inconsistent policies at government level and very few reliable resources available to allow you to work out what you should be doing to manage your finances properly.

Despite thousands of commentators waxing lyrical about millennials and vast numbers of research papers and demographic studies being produced, the world still seems a little confused about the millennial. Polling organisation Ipsos recently published a global survey that lays bare the misperceptions of the millennial generation in society and the workplace (https://www.ipsos.com/ipsos-mori/en-uk/millennial-myths-and-realities). The words most commonly associated with the cohort were:

- Tech-savvy
- Selfish
- Materialistic
- Lazy
- Arrogant

Ouch. It appears the world has a somewhat disapproving view of millennials. What might also surprise you is that this group are also slightly derogatory about themselves! Millennials in the same survey most commonly describe their peers as greedy, selfish and lazy, so aren't showing a great deal of solidarity amongst themselves!

We should not be surprised that the world seems shocked at the new generation. Throughout history, the old have always disapproved of the young. The Earl of Shaftesbury in 1843 said, 'The morals of the young are tenfold worse than formerly'. Ye old media were equally derogatory with a Town and Country magazine letter in 1771 calling the young 'a race of effeminate, self-admiring, emaciated fribbles' which makes the current lexicon look rather mild.

The Ipsos research picks out some surprising trends that go against conventional wisdom about millennials. It shows that British millennials are staying with their employers longer than previous generations did at the same age. This is surprising when we conjure up the image of the bearded hipster freelancing from a café as an example of this generation. Further research from Telefonica and the Financial Times dispel the myth that millennials feel entitled with 45% believing a well-paid job is a privilege and not a right.

What then is the truth about millennials? Well, as you probably guessed, millennials are obsessed with their smartphones. "Millennials are more comfortable with technology than previous generations, having grown up in the era of high-speed internet," according to Michael Clemence, research manager at Ipsos and a co-author of the report.

Millennials spend 1,457 minutes per week on their phones, more than double the figure for Generation X. As the best-educated cohort in history, there is also evidence that university life has made millennials more likely to travel, more open to new experiences and more tolerant of our diverse society.

Less Wealth

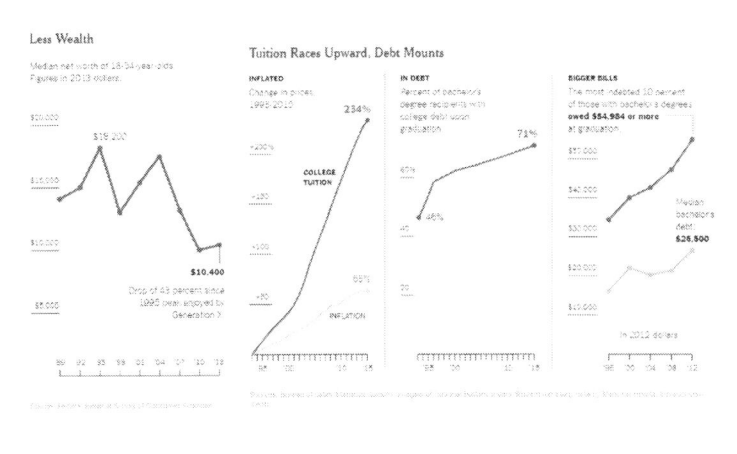

Median net worth of 18-34-year-olds. Figures in 2013 dollars.

$19,200

$10,400

Drop of 43 percent since 1995 peak enjoyed by Generation X

Tuition Races Upward, Debt Mounts

INFLATED
Change in prices, 1995-2015
234%
COLLEGE TUITION
65%
INFLATION

IN DEBT
Percent of bachelor's degree recipients with college debt upon graduation
71%
60%
46%
40%

BIGGER BILLS
The most indebted 10 percent of those with bachelor's degrees owed $54,984 or more at graduation.

Median bachelor's debt
$26,500

In 2012 dollars

Earning Much Less, Despite More Education

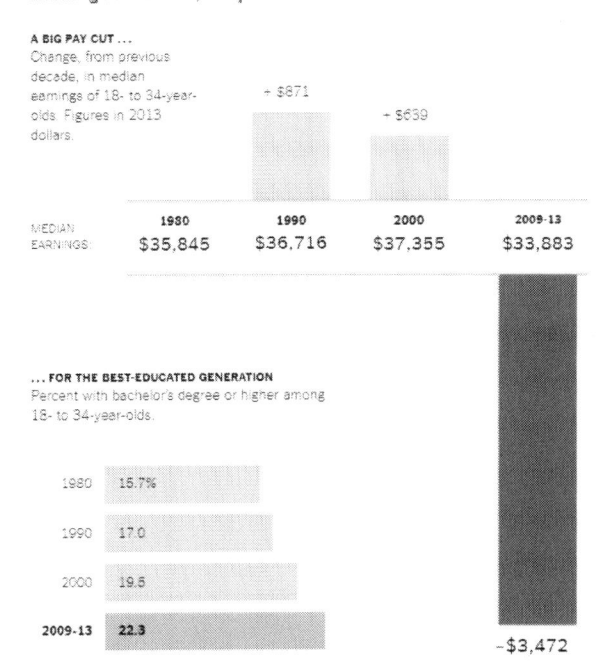

A BIG PAY CUT...
Change, from previous decade, in median earnings of 18- to 34-year-olds. Figures in 2013 dollars.

+ $871

+ $639

MEDIAN EARNINGS	1980	1990	2000	2009-13
	$35,845	$36,716	$37,355	$33,883

... FOR THE BEST-EDUCATED GENERATION
Percent with bachelor's degree or higher among 18- to 34-year-olds.

1980 15.7%
1990 17.0
2000 19.5
2009-13 22.3

-$3,472

Sources: census.gov, censusexplorer; Census Bureau; ipums.org; Minnesota Population Center
Charts by Bill Marsh

What Does the Financial Future Look Like then?

We often take for granted that which is right before us. The change caused by technology is so rampant in our society that it is practically a cliché. This means it is easy to ignore the speed at which disruption is occurring and miss the speed by which this disruption is accelerating. How we manage these new technologies will determine their effect on companies, labour and society.

Artificial intelligence (AI) that automates roles traditionally done by humans will increasingly impact upon the workforce. Jobs that require repetitive tasks will be the first to go followed in the not too distant future by many manufacturing roles.

I remain highly optimistic about the positive benefits of AI on society. During my working life, I have worked hard to help develop the use of AI to allow the average financial adviser to complete many of their tasks ten times faster. This means they can help ten times more people manage their finances. Advisers will be able to spend their time doing what they do best, speaking with customers and building relationships, instead of being bogged down in administration. This concept of man and machine working in partnership to radically improve efficiency and lower costs for customers is one which will play out across all industries. In order to flourish in this new world, it is therefore essential that the modern workforce develop the technical skills to interact and work in harmony with AI.

In a research report in 2015, Deloitte University's Leadership Centre for Inclusion showed that millennials are already in positions of authority within the workplace with

41% having four or more direct reports, which is significantly higher than Gen Xers at the same age. This shows that despite financial headwinds, millennials are gaining valuable management experience and climbing the corporate ladder which can be helpful when looking for additional ways to increase income which we will come to later.

One huge factor that millennials have in their favour is an affinity with technology that no previous generation has ever had. Recent research from credit rating agency Moodys, shows that 90% of millennials check their smartphone within 15 minutes of waking, and the average person has more information at their fingertips than the President of the United States did in the 1970s. This transparency and access to information have profound effects on society at all levels from politics to commerce.

A three-year study in the USA from Scratch, an in-house unit of Viacom, found that one in three millennials is open to switching banks in the next 90 days, something the previous generation did every decade. Through price comparison sites and smart apps, millennials are now more price sensitive than any other generation and expect the best deal when buying. An IRI survey (https://www.iriworldwide.com/IRI/media/Key-Trends_Q2-2017t.pdf) found that seven out of ten millennials generally buy the lowest price item whilst grocery shopping, as compared to 59% of adults overall.

People today remain a confident and resilient in a world which is changing faster than at any time in history. Research Conducted by America's SBDC in 2017 found that, 61% of millennials believe that the best job security comes from owning your own business. This increased ability to challenge the status quo and leverage technology to build and test new businesses that disrupt traditional industries will be a key driver of economic development in the future. Increasingly, unhappy with the world of work they are in, people are taking charge and shaping their future. Expect the future of work driven by tech-savvy, entrepreneurial people to look very different from that of today.

However, finances remain an area where, unlike other aspects of their lives, millennials struggle to make the most of the money that they have accumulated.

Sameer Aurora, the head of client strategy for UBS Wealth Management Americas, found in a 2016 research study that even though they have a longer investment window, millennials hold almost twice as much cash in their portfolios as baby boomers. This shows that contrary to previous generations, they prefer physical assets as well as cash when investing their money even when this delivers a lower return.

This aversion to risk can have disastrous consequences for long-term saving as the money we invest is not working as hard for us as it potentially could do. We will return to this topic in our chapter on investing.

Although Americans currently aged between 30 and 39 are calculated to have amassed 46% less wealth as of 2017 than the equivalent cohort in 2007, we should not forget how far things have come since the financial crisis. Unemployment is at an all-time low; we are seeing economies grow across the globe and interest rates rising for the first time in a decade which will help savers. Much of the panic around sovereign nations going bust has also disappeared, meaning banks are lending more to small businesses which will help fuel much of the entrepreneurial endeavours of the current generation.

In the UK, where skyrocketing house prices have driven intergenerational unfairness, millennial policies that focus on helping this generation are climbing up the priority list as politicians seek to attract this powerful voter group. Many millennials have found their voice since the outcome of the referendum on European Union membership (younger generations voted overwhelmingly for 'remain', whilst older voters tended to favour 'Brexit'). Following this outcome, to appease the younger generations, the Conservative government introduced measures to help young people get onto the housing ladder by cutting stamp duty – a tax on purchases – for many first-time buyers.

Although voter turnout rates tend to be higher amongst baby boomers, millennials are set to be the biggest and most powerful political force in the developed world. As a warning to established political structures, Ipsos research shows millennials in many countries are less likely to be loyal to a particular party than their predecessors, which means politicians will have to devise incentives to earn and keep their votes. These younger voters are not afraid to push their own agenda. If we take the example of Greta Thunberg, love her or hate her, you can't underestimate the power and reach she has achieved in just a few years. In May 2019, Thunberg was featured on the cover of Time magazine, was featured in a 30-minute Vice documentary titled Make the World Greta Again, was made an honorary fellow of the Royal Scottish Geographical Society and was named by Time as one of the 100 most influential people in the world. We should also not neglect to mentioned that she is the youngest individual Time Person of the Year and that after addressing the UN Climate Action Summit in New York, she was nominated for the 2019 Nobel Peace Prize. Amazing the impact someone can have with a little protesting and marketing expertise.

Despite those in work today still suffering some of the aftershocks of the financial crisis, there is a real reason to feel more confident about the future of our finances.

Although many have had a tough start in their careers and may well be derided by older generations, it is this generation's ability to harness technology and innovate that will drive progress. People today have never had more data in which to aid decision making or low-cost professional services that help them plan for the future. We should all have real confidence that regardless of where we are at with our finances, we have the tools available to us to make real long-term positive changes.

Chapter 4

'When I was young I thought that money was the most important thing in life; now that I am old I know that it is'.
–Oscar Wilde

Millionaire Mindset

'The number one reason most people don't get what they want is that they don't know what they want.' – T. Harv Eker

Ma Yun was born on the 10th September 1964 in Zhejiang, China. Ma's parents were traditional musicians from China, who also did some storytelling in order to support their family. The family would have been considered poor, but Ma's upbringing was a happy one.

What May lacked in money he made up for with drive and determination. Seeing wealthy foreigners at the upmarket Hangzhou International Hotel and sensing an opportunity, he began studying English at a young age and bolstered his lessons by conversing with the English-speaking hotel guests. Ma quickly turned his language skills into a business and for 9 years would ride 17 miles on his bicycle to give tours of the area for tourists to practice his English. He became pen pals with one of those foreigners, who nicknamed him 'Jack' because he found it hard to pronounce his Chinese name.

Despite working hard to improve his English, Ma struggled to get into college. The Chinese entrance exams are held only once a year and Ma took 4 years to pass. Ma attended Hangzhou Teacher's Institute and graduated in 1988 with a Bachelor of Arts in English.

After graduation, he applied for 30 jobs and got rejected from all of them. He tells a story where KFC came to his town and they interviewed 24 people. Twenty-three of them got the job and he was the unlucky one. Ma's persistence paid off and he eventually became a lecturer in English and international trade at Hangzhou Dianzi University. During this period he also applied ten times to Harvard Business School and got rejected each time.

In 1994, Ma heard about the internet and sensed an early opportunity as China had little online coverage. He founded a company called Chinapages.com and within 3 years he had generated revenue of $800,000 and gained the interest of several investors.

From 1998 to 1999, Ma headed an information technology company established by the China International Electronic Commerce Centre, a department of the Ministry of Foreign Trade and Economic Cooperation. However, stifled by the bureaucracy of the government organisation, in 1999, he quit and returned to Hangzhou with his team to found Alibaba, a China-based business-to-business marketplace site.

In his apartment with a group of 18 friends, Ma set his sights on the goal of being the eBay of China. This was no small task as eBay itself was already trying to break into the Chinese market. Ma instilled a working day of 9-9-6 or 9am to 9pm 6 days a week. He credits this laser focus and dedication for the reason why today Alibaba is worth $600 billion, and he is one of the richest people on the planet.

Do you know what your goals are? Not what you 'hope for' or 'wish for' but solid goals with associated actions, time frames and consequences. Do these goals match your daily activities and habits?

With a little introspection and asking yourself these simple questions, you should be able to begin to tease out the behaviours and beliefs that are getting in the way of you achieving what you want.

Without fail, every one of the experts in their field used for this book were fanatical about developing a mindset that gave them the best possible chance of success. We all have bad habits when it comes to our finances. Whether spending too much on nights out or forgetting to put money aside every month as soon as we are paid, these are the habits that sabotage our ability to build wealth.

Neal and Wood in their paper, 'A new look at habits and the habit-goal interface', defined habits as actions that are triggered automatically in response to contextual cues that have been associated with their performance: for example, automatically washing hands (action) after using the toilet (contextual cue) or putting on a seatbelt (action) after getting into the car (contextual cue). Decades of psychological research consistently show that mere repetition of a simple action in a consistent context leads, through associative learning, to the action being activated upon subsequent exposure to those contextual cues.

We are all creatures of habit, and anything that we encounter that falls outside of our normal daily routine can be annoying and stressful. I am guessing that one of the reasons you are reading this book is that you are looking to change or improve something. For this book to have any impact on your life, it will require a mindset shift; otherwise, you will go back to old patterns of behaviour.

Knowledge is nothing without action. If we are honest with ourselves, we can all pinpoint certain habits which are self-destructive, and we should stop, for example, spending money online (action) after seeing an advert for shoes (contextual cue). What would it take to rewire these habits into something more positive?

We all know that we should get off the sofa, turn the TV off, throw down that bar of chocolate and embrace life. You probably also know that you could do more at work to progress, should plan your time better and prioritise tasks that are driving you towards your goals.

However, if you are like the average person in the street, you keep putting off that which you know you should be doing today. In other words, there is a huge gap between the knowledge you have and the actions you choose to take.

What is it then that creates this gap?

Are You Afraid to Change?

Failure can be a crutch. Failure when trying something new gives you permission to go back to your comfort zone. After all, you tried your best, and it didn't work so best go back to what you were doing before, right? Failure represents a continuation of a routine which will always be easier than change. Perversely, this failure can give us pleasure. For example, when we try a new diet and quickly fail to stick to it by picking up that biscuit, we are giving in to that short-term pleasure at the expense of our longer-term goal.

We know that the endless pursuit of pleasure will be unlikely to lead to long-term happiness and when we chase short-term pleasure such as eating badly, drinking too much or even sitting browsing Facebook for hours, we are sabotaging our future happiness. The realisation that all we are doing is exchanging short-term pleasure for long-term unhappiness might provide the key to changing some of these habits.

Pleasure and happiness are very different things. Since Aristotle, happiness has been usefully thought of as consisting of at least two aspects: hedonia (pleasure) and eudaimonia (a life well lived). In contemporary psychology these aspects are usually referred to as pleasure and meaning.

Pleasure provides us with momentary feelings of happiness, but this happiness is fleeting and doesn't last long as it is wholly dependent upon external events and experiences. Once these events and experiences end, so does the pleasure, and this encourages us, like junkies, to chase the next short-term high. This short-termism is what allows us to put off planning towards our long-term goals which are where real, long-lasting happiness lives.

A Princeton University study conducted on students asked them to consider delayed reward problems whilst undergoing functional magnetic resonance imaging (fMRI), a procedure that shows the parts of the brain that are always active. The students were offered choices between Amazon.com gift certificates ranging from $5 to $40 in value and larger amounts that could be obtained only by waiting for some period, from two weeks to six weeks. In other words, they wanted to see what the brain was up to when considering delayed gratification or sacrificing short-term pleasure for longer-term happiness.

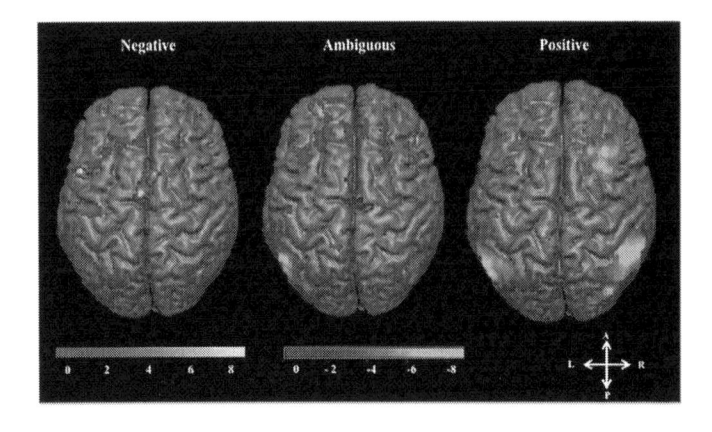

Three-dimensional surface projections of activations (e.g. PosImprov > PosChrom) and deactivations (e.g. PosChrom > PosImprov) during improvisation for different emotion conditions

Source: Limb et al./Scientific Reports

The study showed that decisions involving the possibility of immediate reward activated parts of the brain influenced heavily by neural systems associated with emotion. Most importantly, when students had the choice of an immediate reward but chose the delayed option, the calculating regions of their brains were more strongly activated than their emotional systems.

Having an awareness of our emotions is a key first step towards altering our mindset. Give it a go. Try writing down a list of all your activities for just one day. How much time did you spend completing tasks that move you towards your longer-term goals versus allowing yourself to be distracted? How many of your actions were driven by emotional needs versus planned activities aimed at achieving longer-term objectives? What will you do differently tomorrow to change this?

Are You All Talk and No Action?

As the saying goes, 'Talk is cheap'. Talking about your problems is a great way of working out what action you should be taking and getting your head in the right place, but unless it leads to tangible action, then it is effectively pointless.

We all have that friend who before they do anything will need to speak with several people to validate what they are doing. These 'askholes' will then often choose to ignore any advice that they have been given and go about doing what they were before.

Talking about problems to death rarely solves them. It is understandable that when confronting a new experience or life-changing event that you want to have all the correct information at your disposal but sometimes you just have to take the plunge and get on with it.

The next time you feel the urge to validate one of your decisions with someone else, try just doing it. If you've learnt the basics of what you are about to do, get on with it. If you succeed, it will boost your confidence in your decision-making ability and intuition far more than if you got that external validation. If it fails, then look at the results and adjust your future efforts accordingly. Way too much time is spent on navel-gazing and contemplating starting something. Just dive in, the worst that can happen is rarely long lasting.

If you have never written a to-do list, give it a go now. Once you have emptied your brain into a list, look for things that you have been putting off for some time that can be achieved in under 30 minutes. Rank them in order of priority. Complete as many of these 30-minute jobs in one day as you can. Any 30-minute task left at the end of the day should be deleted. If you haven't done it up until now despite it only taking 30 minutes and it's not high on your priority list, it probably doesn't need doing, so free up some mental energy and cast it aside.

You Rely on Motivation Instead of Creating a Habit

Monday mornings are tough. You have had two days off for the weekend and broken your routine and must start fresh. This is completely normal and happens to everyone. If you find yourself always having to mentally push yourself to get out of bed on time, go to the gym, eat healthily or any other positive action and then you probably haven't devoted the time to creating habits and are relying solely on motivation. Motivation will wax and wane; habits are instinctual.

Lewis Howes who runs an amazing podcast and is an X Pro football player turned seven-figure lifestyle entrepreneur, business coach, keynote speaker and author is aware of the power of habits to drive long-term results. He is focused on the perfect morning habits to drive success throughout his day.

'I start with gratitude. Right when I wake up, I think about what I'm most grateful for that day. Then I either do a simple-guided meditation or ground myself in what my intention is for the day. I think about the most important things I want to accomplish.

I am a big believer in making my bed every morning. It's something simple I can do for myself that starts my day off with accomplishment. After that I do a workout, sometimes running, lifting, kickboxing or meeting up with a friend for a workout. This is important to me, even when I'm on the road. I make a green smoothie or juice and take a shower, and then I get after my day'. Life does not simply happen to us. It is an output of the choices that we make and the actions that we take. We all have that friend who seems to always be late, loses their phone, has long strings of bad luck and is always ill or has some grumble about their health. They never seem to be organised, and life pushes them around.

In Jocko's case, his habits effectively tell him what to do as soon as his alarm clock goes off. He doesn't lie there waiting to see if his inbuilt motivation will get him up. He has a routine, and he sticks to it and a plan that he is focused on achieving. Try pre-planning your mornings in detail before you go to bed for just one week. See what a difference it can make when you rely on habit rather than motivation.

You Accept Your Excuses

In a fixed mindset, people believe their qualities are fixed traits, and nothing they do can change that. For example, you believe your naturally bad at maths or shy or that you will never be athletic. People in a fixed mindset document their intelligence and talents and, as they see them as static, don't see the value in working to develop and improve them. They also believe that talent alone leads to success, and effort is not required.

Alternatively, in a growth mindset, people have an inbuilt belief that knowledge, capability and intelligence can grow over time and be improved with experience. Individuals with a growth mindset believe that they can get smarter and that performance is directly related to the effort that they put in. Generally, once in this mindset, these people will put in extra effort, leading to higher achievement.

This concept was first developed by Carol Dweck and was discussed in detail in her book, Mindset. 'For twenty years, my research has shown that the view you adopt of yourself profoundly affects the way you lead your life'.

The example that Dweck uses in her book sums up the thought processes that you will find in growth versus fixed mindsets.

'One day, you go to a class that is important to you and that you like a lot. The professor returns the midterm papers to the class. You got a C+. You're very disappointed. That evening on the way back to your home, you find that you've gotten a parking ticket. Being frustrated, you call your best friend to share your experience but are brushed off.

How would you respond? What would you think? If you thought, 'What a crummy day. I would feel like a failure. I would be frustrated. I wouldn't feel motivated to study for the final exam. Maybe I'm just bad at that class', then you may tend towards the fixed mindset. If you thought, 'Well, I probably shouldn't have parked there. And maybe my friend had a bad day? I'll have to study harder for the final', then you may tend towards the growth mindset.

This fixed versus growth mindset is incredibly important in how we view our finances. If we make the excuse that the reason we are in debt, don't earn the money we want or miss a promotion is all because of where we went to school, how our parents treated us, our background or our ethnicity, and that this can't be changed, then we will never improve. If you make these excuses and allow yourself to accept them, then you will never be able to change your behaviour.

Self-help guru, Tony Robbins, suggests that if we are going to blame external events for our current situation, then blame them fully! That crappy parenting you received is to blame for you being a more compassionate and caring parent yourself. The intolerance about your race is to blame for that deep reserve of passion and hunger that gives you the energy to overcome anything and prove people wrong. That school you went to is to blame for your ability to work in conditions that make most feel uncomfortable. Blame these things but blame them fully.

So which category do you fit into? And which category do you think will lead you to long-term success and happiness? Are you a hedonist like our 'lotto lout' Michael, an innovator and entrepreneur like Mark or a careful and considered financial planner like Lidia? Do you believe if you are in one category or the other that you are powerless to switch?

You Give up Before You even Start

Once we pull our heads out of the sand and realise just how far away from our goals and how much action is needed, we are likely to feel a little daunted. At this point, some of us will quit and go back to the life we had. Others will summon the strength to act and do what is required. Whether finances, relationships or our health, the strength of the motivation needed to act is what will drive the success of what we are trying to achieve. When the shit hits the fan, are you going to look into the abyss and see the whole process as hopeless or are you the sort of person who can handle radical change and get on track for the life you have always wanted?

In his book the *7 Habits of Highly Effective People*, which has sold almost 20 million copies in 38 languages, Steven Covey recommends that we adopt the habit to 'begin with the end in mind'.

Unless you have a clear picture of where you would like to be financially and in what time frame you are highly unlikely to take steps to get there, ask yourself right now, are you where you want to be financially? Are you where you dreamed you'd be at this age? Be honest; this is only yourself you are talking to!

Well now is as good a time as any to act. On a piece of paper, write down the top three things that you would like to achieve with your finances in the next 30 days, 365 days, 1,825 days (5 years) and 3,650 days (10 years). Be as creative as possible. This is not a time to limit yourself; write down as much as you can and force yourself to carry out this task for at least 15 minutes.

Hopefully, you have a big list of hairy, audacious goals. Great! Pin them up somewhere you will get to see them every day. We want these goals burned into your subconscious, so they subtly impact your daily actions.

As Covey talks about in his book, all things are created twice, first in your mind and then through your actions as they are brought into the physical world. The physical creation follows the mental, just as a building follows a blueprint. The reason we write down these goals and push ourselves to think big is that we want to put ourselves firmly in that growth mindset camp. If you have a goal, a plan and the will to do whatever it takes to achieve it, you will get where you want to go.

If you don't make a conscious effort to visualise where you want to get to and what you hope to achieve in your life, then you will float around at the whim of others who have a firm vision of what they want out of their lives. Starting with the end in mind gives you an anchor for your future decisions. You can view whatever decisions life throws at you against your end goal, and by doing so, you will find solutions to difficult decisions come very easily.

Altering your attitude towards money is very similar to altering your attitude towards your health. There are thousands of weight loss programs many of which claim miracle results, but without fail, none of them will work unless the individual has made a conscious decision to change how they live.

At age 45, Keith Ahrens was living in Las Vegas and tipping the scales at over 400 pounds. He didn't exercise, ate huge portions of unhealthy food and hadn't seen a doctor in years.

However, on a fateful day in 2007, he found himself with shortness of breath, dizziness and nausea that was so bad he finally bit the bullet and went to the doctor. This visit saved his life. Keith was having a heart attack and needed a triple-bypass operation.

'When I was told I needed open-heart surgery to save my life, the room seemed dark', Keith recalls. 'I remember feeling like I had let everyone down. I felt like I had let myself down. As I lay there I kept thinking over and over, how could I have let this happen to myself?'

After enduring open-heart surgery, Keith survived and made a promise to himself to turn around his unhealthy lifestyle. Keith lost half his body weight and now acts as a spokesperson for the American Heart Association, sharing his story to help others avoid the denial that almost killed him. You can learn more about Keith's incredible story and how he has gone on to help more people just like him at https://keithahrens.com/ The secret to Keith's success was breaking his bad habits. This involved immediately cutting out sodas and visits to fast-food restaurants. He didn't try any fad diets or quick fixes; instead he set out to learn about sustainable heart-healthy eating he could work on every day. He started walking regularly for exercise and set small, achievable goals such as to move more each day. The real key was that he didn't try and change everything at once but took small steps towards a long-term goal of better health.

How many times have you sat down and developed a diet plan for yourself which involved cutting out all sugar, turning vegan and going to the gym seven days a week all from a standing start? I would argue these wild lifestyle changes are doomed to fail as they require too much change in too little time. Look for incremental improvements and start them immediately.

Keith's story is typical of people who experience large shifts in perception. In this case, it took him almost dying to jolt him into action. Key to his success was keeping things simple, not looking for a quick fix and simply building upon his daily successes.

After graduating college Chris Reining took a job in corporate America. A few years later, after saving some money, he bought a little condo to live in and BMW to drive.

He was living the American dream. However, one day, sitting in his drab cubicle at work, he thought, 'So I have to do this 40 more years?'

Much like Keith, Chris had let little daily habits build up and bloat his monthly expenditure to the point where he wasn't saving much and was faced with a life that didn't excite him.

Like Keith's heart attack, Chris' revelation whilst sitting in his cubicle was the point in his life where he decided to take action. It took time but Chris worked his way up to a point where he was saving 54% of his income and developed several different revenue streams, which allowed him to build a $1 million portfolio by age 35. Two years later, Chris officially retired.

Like Keith, Chris started with the small things. 'I know there are some people out there that say you shouldn't worry about the $5 latte, but the more I think about it, cutting out the $5 latte was a good place to start. Because if you try to downsize your house, get rid of all your cars and make all of these drastic changes, it's so overwhelming, and you're not going to do any of it'.

After cutting out his morning coffee, Chris stopped the $15 lunches he bought every day. Next, he targeted his bigger expenditures, all with the long-term goal of financial freedom in his 30s.

'The small changes will lead you to be able to make the big changes', Chris says. Plus, 'you can always go back and add the small changes in later.

It's at this point you must ask yourself what will it take to change the way you manage your money? Is it falling into significant debt? Flirting with or even declaring bankruptcy? Is it arguing about finances with your partner to the point where you break up?

It is very difficult to identify people's triggers for change, and they tend to be unique to us all. Tony Robbins says, 'all personal breakthroughs begin with a change in beliefs'. To finish this section, I want you to reflect on the beliefs you have about money. Which of them can you trace back to your earliest memories? Was there something you can remember from childhood that would have had an impact on the way you view money? Did parents often seem stressed and would argue about making ends meet? It is important to identify which of them come from a fixed mindset and which of them come from a growth mindset. Look at those that come from a fixed mindset and challenge them; try to think creatively around why they may not be true and what course of action you can take today that would begin to break them down.

The Money Life Balance

When you study the thousands of millionaires who have shared their stories, other than those who inherited their wealth, there is never an easy or straightforward path to success. Anyone who tells you otherwise is probably trying to sell you something to line their own pockets, and hopefully, your bullshit radar will ring loud enough to not get scammed!

One ability those who are good with their money have is an appreciation of the Money Life Balance. The Money Life Balance is a simple concept best explained by looking at the two extremes of financial behaviour.

On one end of the spectrum is someone who lives either with a relative or in very uncomfortable accommodation, hoards their money and loathes spending it on anything, eats tinned food, buys second-hand clothes and doesn't socialise due to the cost. This individual is generally miserable and bored; however, they end every month with a large surplus of cash that they squirrel away. For this person, spending money is a constant source of anxiety, and they cling to it as a source of comfort and security. Think of the character Scrooge who rations coal to his employees in the cold depths of winter in order to save money. I think we can assume, although wealthy, he probably doesn't have a healthy relationship with money.

At the other end of the spectrum is someone who loves going out and socialising, is always first to the bar, has the most expensive TV package with all the channels, has the newest phone on the market and loves designer clothes. At the end of the month, this person is generally terrified to check their bank balance and will always be in the red and heavily in debt. Money has very little value to this person and only matters when it inconveniences their lifestyle at which point it causes significant stress and disruption.

These two people represent the two ends of the Money Life Balance. One has money but no life, bearing some similarities to Lidia in the first chapter, and the other has life but no money, think 'lotto lout' Michael. You wouldn't want to be either one of them for any extended period as neither has a healthy relationship with money. Appreciating the concept of the Money Life Balance and where we are on it can tell you a lot about your spending habits and your relationship with money.

If you find yourself on the Scrooge end of the spectrum, you must look deeper into why you gain so much security from money. Do fluctuations in your bank account match the fluctuations in the opinion of your self-worth? If so, you are likely to be overly cautious, and you will be unwilling to take on the kinds of risks that are needed to see your money grow long term. You need to see money as a means to an end and not an emotional crutch or as bestselling author Simon Sinek says, 'Money is not purpose. Money is fuel'.

If you find yourself on the other end of the spectrum, then you can expect to never build up any lasting wealth. As your salary increases, then so will your expenses. A bigger house, a more expensive holiday, more expensive clothes, these trappings can hoover up even the largest of salaries. It is why so many people describe themselves as being trapped in the rat race. Larger salaries beget larger expenses and more liabilities, and neither wealth nor financial resilience is improved. Money should be respected as a tool and used to facilitate longer-term objectives as well as short-term gratification.

To achieve financial freedom, sacrifice and change will be required. You must be comfortable that to save more you must forego some of life's finer things. Like Chris in the last chapter shows, living in the moment is all well and good, but if you have to accept a future where you can't afford to turn the heating on and have to eat baked beans out of a can, then clearly balance has not been achieved.

Therefore, ask yourself, what is the minimum level of comfort you are willing to accept? What areas of your life can you deem luxuries that you only spend money on because it is what is expected of you? Every time you feel the need to upgrade from this base level of expenditure, think about what you are giving up in the future to do so.

The Money Life Balance is a key concept when trying to build your own Money Triangle. If your earnings are only allowing you to live a life where you are only just covering the essentials, you know that you must do more to add additional sources of income or increase what you currently earn for what you are doing to add balance to your Triangle.

One of the best ways to decide where you are comfortable being on the Money Life Balance is to go back to your list of financial goals that you have stuck up on the wall from our Millionaire Mindset chapter. How many of those goals are achieved when you show off by buying a big bottle of vodka at some club where everyone is there just to be seen? Does the latest iPhone which will be obsolete within a year or two help you get where you want to go? Does having the full sports package on TV distract you from finding your next business idea as well as taking much-needed money out of your pocket?

By regularly referring to your goals, it helps you stay laser focused on want you want to achieve and not what others will try and influence you to do. Having clear goals allows you to shut out the external noise of peers and advertisers who all want to pull you in a different direction and not necessarily help you achieve what you have put down on your plan.

Now is a good time to go back to the financial goals that you wrote down earlier. It is time to dig a little deeper. To know why you want to achieve each one of these. Not just a surface reason, but the deep emotional driver behind it. Don't stop until you have at least three why's for each of your financial goals. We want to start putting some powerful reasoning behind our plan.

For example:

I want to be debt free by the time I am 40.

Why?

- I am sick and tired of the interest payments from my loan, meaning I am in my overdraft at the end of the month.
- I would feel more relaxed, confident and in control of my finances if I didn't have debt hanging over me, and this would make me less short-tempered and a nicer person to be around.
- Added security from paying off my debt would give me the confidence to look at more speculative investments that are likely to gain in value more than money just sitting in the bank

I want to own a 10-bed house in a beautiful countryside location.

Why?

- It will make me feel like I have made it. It is a physical manifestation of my success.
- It will provide an amazing place for my family to grow and relax and give them added security.
- Having a home that I never plan to sell will give me a feeling of security and stability.

I want to have a passive income of more than £1 million per year.

Why?

- Earning more than I will ever need even if I choose not to work will give me a sense of financial freedom.
- Not having enough money is stressful. I want the security that whatever happens, I will be ok.
- I want to be able to provide for my family and give them whatever they want.

This is just a small selection of some of my early goals which have evolved considerably over time. What I found extremely useful when analysing what I wrote down was picking out the recurring themes. It's obvious that there was a recurring theme of status and I was tying money very closely with security for both myself and my family. I also seem to link money and materialistic possessions closely with personal satisfaction and happiness. This can be dangerous and lead to an unhealthy relationship with money and may not lead to the sort of happiness we would expect.

Numerous studies have been done on happiness, and the results vary enormously. Rarely though do materialistic ambitions feature anywhere in what drives long-term happiness.

Harvard University conducted an almost 80-year study on 268 Harvard sophomores starting in 1938 to look specifically at what factors contributed to living longer and achieving happiness. The study found that close relationships, more than money or fame, are what keep people happy throughout their lives. Close relationships protect people from life's ups and downs, help to delay mental and physical decline and are better predictors of long and happy lives than social class, IQ or even genes.

Mo Gawdat, previously Google's Chief Business Officer, made the study of happiness his passion when in 2014 his son Ali lost his life to a preventable medical error during a simple surgical procedure. 'Solve For Happy' is Mo's mission to deliver his happiness message to one billion people around the world. His algorithm is extremely simple:

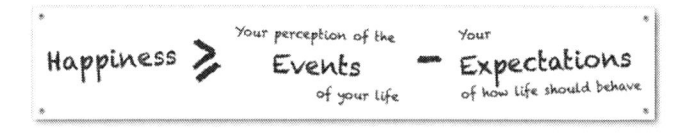

$$\text{Happiness} \geq \text{Your perception of the Events of your life} - \text{Your Expectations of how life should behave}$$

Source: www.solveforhappy.com

The higher your ambition or expectations, the better your perception of your life must be for you to feel happy. If you have ever wondered why highly successful, famous and adored people are often amongst the most depressed and miserable, this algorithm might shed some light.

Gaby Hinsliff, who writes for the Guardian paper, noted that the happiest person in her household is unquestionably the dog, precisely because his expectations extend no further than being fed twice a day. Open a sack of dog biscuits, and he's winning. Dogs may aim low, but they pretty much nail it every day as a result.

In a world where we are all connected, and all we see of other people is manicured social media profiles, it can often feel like we are not doing as well as those around us. This has the effect of increasing the size of the right-hand side of Mo's equation leading to us being less happy. Increased social media use has given rise to a self-confidence crisis in many active users and increasing instances of depression. It is important to focus on your own goals instead of constantly comparing yourself to others. Mark Twain summed it up nicely when he said, 'comparison is the death of joy'.

If you are consciously taking small steps each day that, in your mind, are pushing you towards the goals you have set yourself, you can find yourself on the road to real long-term happiness.

Although specific net worth goals still form a key part of my own goals, I have changed the 'why' behind them. Having money is more about the freedom it gives me to try different projects, learn new skills, travel and develop relationships with family and friends. These motivations run far deeper than wanting a bigger salary or better car than an Instagram contact, and when things get tough, these motivations are the cornerstone of my energy to continue. Make sure your list of goals contains your emotional drivers for achieving them. Keep these visible and read them regularly and remember to keep technology firmly in its supporting role.

Who Wants to Be a Millionaire?

Enough preamble show me the damn money!

We have discussed the need for structured solid financial goals, the identification of deeply personal and emotional motivations and a change in mindset. What we now need to start to work out is how we go about achieving your own solid Money Triangle to obtain the outcomes we have talked about.

There are numerous ways to become a millionaire but how fast this happens will depend on the three sides of your money triangle: how much you earn, how much you spend and how the assets you buy appreciate. Finding the optimum balance between these three will drive your success. Unsurprisingly, you may also see that this is how we have broken this book down to cover each of these crucial steps.

What is a realistic time frame for achieving financial freedom? Well sadly there is no hard and fast rule, and it will completely depend on your circumstances. The key though is to have a financial plan that leads to a financial outcome that inspires you, which you can then adjust as hopefully your earnings, spending habits and investment returns improve.

Let's start at the beginning. Where are you currently at?

Let's do a quick and dirty calculation of when you will become a millionaire if you change nothing now. For this, we will need a savings calculator. I like the Money Advice Service Calculator which can be found at https://moneyadviceservice.org.uk/en/tools/savings-calculator.

Alternatively, just Google it and you will get loads of fairly accurate results.

To calculate when you will become a millionaire, you will need a few bits of information:

1. How much do you currently have saved?
2. How much are you investing monthly?
3. What investment return are you getting?

Numbers 1 and 2 are fairly easy to answer. Make sure you include all pension contributions made by both you and your employer. Number 3 is slightly tougher; if your investments are sitting in the bank, you can expect an investment return of around 0.5%–1.5% each year. If they are sitting in stocks and shares, then you would hope for long-term growth of around 6%–7% each year.

What is the result? Depressing? Reassuring? If you own a home and are paying off a mortgage, you may wish to add this to your figures, but you will need somewhere to live when you are older so don't necessarily rely on this to make you wealthy.

Try playing around with the calculator; try adding more to the amount you invest or changing the investment return. You should quickly see that these two levers make a massive difference to your outcome.

Let's take a millennial who is 30 years old and has never invested before. If she wanted to have a pot worth £1m plus at the point of retirement, currently 68 in the UK, how much would she need to contribute monthly?

If we assume that she can invest her money at a return of 6%, she would need to contribute £600 per month.

This would lead to a pot of around £1.12m at the point of retirement. This is assuming that there is no tax on the investment returns that she is making, so in the case of someone in the UK, this would be an investment in a pension or in the USA a 401(k). We will come onto these in future chapters.

One major factor that impacts your ability to build wealth is time. As you will see from the table below, if you are retiring at 68, the earlier you start, the easier this is.

Age you started investing	Years to retirement	Yearly return	Monthly investment amount needed to hit £1 million
20	48	6%	324.80
21	47	6%	345.64
22	46	6%	367.90
23	45	6%	391.71
24	44	6%	417.17
25	43	6%	444.43
26	42	6%	473.62
27	41	6%	504.90
28	40	6%	538.46
29	39	6%	574.48
30	38	6%	613.18
31	37	6%	654.79
32	36	6%	699.57
33	35	6%	747.82
34	34	6%	799.87
35	33	6%	856.08

By starting five years earlier, the amount you need to invest each month to hit £1 million drops by almost £170. This shows time is a huge factor, and the cost of delay can make hitting your target almost impossible.

The reason time makes such a huge difference is due to compound interest. A friend of mine Oliver Payne, who oversees the Ford Motor Company's pension schemes in Europe, uses a simple example to explain compound interest, 'if you were to fold a piece of paper 42 times it would reach the Moon'.

What About the Investment Return that We Are Expecting?

If we take that same 30-year-old and increase the annual return by just 1%, the amount she would need to save monthly to hit £1 million goes down by £130. This shows us that one of our major wealth drivers alongside time is investment return.

We will talk further on how to achieve better returns on our money in our 'How to Invest It' chapter, but it is always disheartening to see how many people don't choose to invest their money but leave it in a bank account. Let's say the lady in our example chose to leave her money in the bank at the current interest rate of 1% (this is quite generous as most banks pay a fraction of this). She would need to contribute a staggering £1,000 per month to get to millionaire status in the same time frame.

The approach to building wealth need not be complicated. It will not happen tomorrow, but given consistent behavioural change, you can build a realistic plan of when it *will* happen. No hoping for cryptocurrency riches, no hoping for crazy property investment returns, but building a plan that relies upon tried and tested methodologies that have been used for decades. There will be ups and downs but building a plan is the first step.

You may be drawing a blank at this point as you have no idea what investment return you are currently getting or indeed how much you are investing. Now is the time to find out. Hopefully, you are aware if you have any direct payments coming out of your account into investments, but you also need to check with your employer if you have a pension or other investment product what amount is currently being contributed. Your provider will have issued you a statement that details the yearly return of this product. Finding these things out is important as making adjustments now, as we can see from the previous table, can make a huge difference in the long term.

You may also be sitting there thinking I am full of shit. You have no money to spare because of rent, food bills, travel expenses, etc. so all of this is just a pipe dream. You don't earn enough to get by let alone save money. You are not alone; I hear this a lot when doing seminars trying to help people get into a savings habit. However, I am still yet to find anyone who, once we have dug deeper, didn't have room for improvement. If you are in this mindset, then the next section is for you. It focuses on how anyone, regardless of earnings, can optimise their spending and build a savings habit that gets them on the road to building long-term wealth.

How to Spend It

'Advertising Has Us Chasing Cars And Clothes, Working Jobs We Hate So We Can Buy S*#T We Don't Need'.
– Tyler Durden

In 2010, there was a major change at the team Sky Cycling HQ with the appointment of Dave Brailsford as the new General Manager and Performance Director. Brailsford had a simple task – build a team that would win the Tour De France.

Brailsford was born in the small village of Shardlow in Derbyshire before moving with his family to Wales where he attended school and learnt to speak Welsh. His passion for cycling grew from family holidays spent in France where he was introduced to the sport and showed early promise.

At the point of his appointment to Team Sky, no British cycling team had ever won the Tour de France, and it was Brailsford's job to radically overhaul the team's approach and change history. No small task.

Brailsford spent some of his early career working as an export sales manager at Yorkshire Bike importer and distributor Planet X Bikes. He was first employed by British Cycling as an advisor in 1997 following four years as an amateur cyclist in France.

Brailsford believed in a concept that he referred to as the 'aggregation of marginal gains'. He explained it as 'the 1% margin for improvement in everything you do'. Put simply, if you improve every area related to cycling by just 1%, then those small gains would add up to remarkable improvements and results over time.

Brailsford went about his task with scientific rigour and was known for his emphasis on constantly measuring and monitoring key statistics such as cyclists' power output and developing training interventions that targeted any observed weaknesses.

He started where you might expect by looking at the nutrition of riders, and how they went about their training and then targeted their equipment looking at the ergonomics and aerodynamics of the bike even down to the weight of the tires.

This is typically where the other teams entering the Tour de France would end their process improvement. However, team Sky kept analysing, measuring and testing more holistic elements of the rider's life to look for more 1% improvements wherever they could be found. For example, a key element in the gruelling Tour de France was the ability of the riders to recover between races. It was during this analysis that they found that optimising which pillow riders slept on could improve sleep and taking a favourite pillow with them to hotels could improve recovery. They tested and improved the post-ride recovery anti-inflammatory gels and massage techniques and even taught riders how to best wash to avoid germs and sickness, all the time picking up those 1% incremental improvements to the overall system that others overlooked.

In 2012, Team Sky rider Sir Bradley Wiggins became the first British cyclist to win the Tour de France. That same year, Brailsford coached the British cycling team at the 2012 Olympic Games and dominated the competition by winning 70% of the gold medals available.

2013 went much the same way as 2012 with Team Sky winning the Tour de France with rider Chris Froome. Many have referred to the British cycling feats in the Olympics and the Tour de France as the most successful run in modern cycling history.

What is the key message here?

Simply put, penny-pinching does add up! Like Team Sky, if you can improve individual spending habits by just 1% in multiple areas of your life, it will quickly add up to large sums of money as, for example, each £50 per month saved by a 30-year-old is worth £87,000 at aged 68.

James Clear is the author of the bestselling book Atomic Habits and is on a mission to answer the question: 'How can we live better?' He analyses how small habit changes can have huge long-term impacts.

'It's so easy to overestimate the importance of one defining moment and underestimate the value of making better decisions on a daily basis.

Almost every habit that you have — good or bad — is the result of many small decisions over time.

And yet, how easily we forget this when we want to make a change.

So often we convince ourselves that change is only meaningful if there is some large, visible outcome associated with it. Whether it is losing weight, building a business, travelling the world or any other goal, we often put pressure on ourselves to make some earth-shattering improvement that everyone will talk about.

Meanwhile, improving by just 1 per cent isn't notable (and sometimes it isn't even noticeable). But it can be just as meaningful, especially in the long run'.

Just as these incremental 1% improvements can have a huge positive impact on your finances, the reverse is also true. This can be summed up by the following graph:

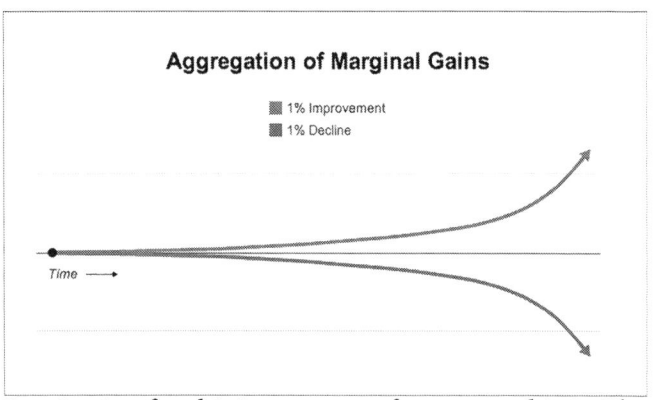

Aggregation of Marginal Gains

■ 1% Improvement
■ 1% Decline

Time ⟶

Inspiration for this image came from a graphic in The Slight Edge by Jeff Olson.

You can see that the compounding nature of these marginal improvements has little impact at the start of the journey; however, they really build up over the long term. Consistency is the key to grasping the power of the 1% rule. We should all look at our actions daily and ask ourselves 'Where are the marginal gains?' This doesn't have to be just in finance; it could be the decision to take the stairs instead of the lift or take a second to appreciate a view on your way to work. All of these when done consistently over time take very little effort but can make dramatic differences to your life.

The American entrepreneur Jim Rohn summed this up nicely:

'Success is a few simple disciplines, practised every day, whilst failure is simply a few errors in judgment, repeated every day.'

You're Spending more than You Think

When I speak to people about saving more money, the most common response I get is 'I can't afford it' or 'how am I supposed to save more when I am being crushed by my student loan/rent/travel expenses'. I fully appreciate that, for many of us, money is extremely tight and there doesn't seem to be any room in your finances; however, I am still to meet any person who is 100% on top of their spending.

Mike Tyson holds the record as the youngest boxer to win a heavyweight title at 20 years, 4 months and 22 days old. Iron Mike won his first 19 professional fights by knockout, 12 of them in the first round. Throughout his 20-year boxing career, he earned a staggering $400 million according to the New York Times.

Despite these huge earnings, he found himself in serious financial trouble with his extravagant spending, bad business decisions and divorce eventually catching up with him. According to Business Insider, when the former heavyweight champion filed for bankruptcy in 2003, he was $23 million in debt. His debts included a $9 million divorce settlement, $13.4 million in US taxes, and $4 million in British taxes.

Mike was known for his extravagant spending and, according to therichest.com, allegedly purchased three white Bengal tigers at the height of his fame. Each tiger cost $70,000 to buy, and an additional $200,000 per year in food. That's over $1500 a day in meat! Tyson also apparently hired an animal trainer at the cost of $125,000 a year to take care of them whenever Tyson was in Las Vegas.

As Tyson's story shows, without having some sort of control over what you spend, it is easy to blow through any amount of money so controlling your spending is key to increasing your overall wealth.

The money we have leftover at the end of every day, week or month will determine our options going forward. It is pointless talking about the other two sides of the Money Triangle (increasing your earnings or how to invest your money) if you don't have control of your spending and have nothing left after you receive your pay check. That is why we are starting on the spending side of the Money Triangle.

What follows is a list of good habits that you should have that will ensure you retain as much of the money you earn as possible. The following list is not exhaustive and there are always eagle-eyed observers who can spot a clever way to cut down on spending, but these tend to be the worst offenders when I am speaking with people looking to improve their financial future. If you can find the elusive 1% improvement in each of these segments, then I guarantee you will begin to have options with your money that you have never had before and will get on the road to building wealth through a solid money triangle.

Budgeting

You should consider making a budget if you are:

- Earning limited money
- Trying to lighten your debt load and solve your debt problem
- Working towards a financial goal
- Planning to retire early
- Trying to make the best use of your money

That covers pretty much everyone!

Writing a budget is boring. Sticking to one is incredibly difficult, but it is the best tool to get your finances in order. You will be unlikely to get to the point of financial freedom without one.

Budgeting does not need to be a long and painful process. The simpler you can make it, the more likely you are to follow it.

Proportional budgeting, introduced in the **personal finance** book *All Your Worth*, written by Elizabeth Warren and Amelia Warren Tyagi, is one such simple strategy that can be used to improve your spending.

Take a look at your recent spending. We are now going to split your spending into three categories – needs, saving and wants. Things that fall into the 'needs' category include basic utilities, taxes, mortgage or rent, basic food, basic transportation and insurance. 'Wants' include things like entertainment (cable/Sky above the basic package, Netflix), additional food (super organic, high quality, eating out), extra rent or mortgage for a large home or apartment, extra costs for an expensive vehicle and so on. In other words, anything that goes beyond covering your basic needs. Finally, saving, calculating how much of what you are currently spending is being invested into a pension, other savings plans or any other appreciating asset such as your home.

Once you have analysed where your money is going, it is time to ask yourself if you are happy with the results. Going back to the chapter on mindset, do your spending habits mirror your aspirations? If not, it is time to make some changes.

For example, depending on your level of income, you might want to spend 70% of your money on needs, 15% on wants and 15% on savings. You could describe that as a 70/15/15 budget. If you are just starting out, a good rule of thumb to work out how much you should be saving is to divide your age by two and that's your percentage. For example, if you are 30 years old, you should be saving 15% of your salary. This rule will mean you should be financially independent at the normal retirement age of around 68. If you want to stop working earlier, you will need to save a greater percentage.

The idea with this budget is to revisit it whenever there is a change in your circumstances. When we receive a bonus or a pay rise, there is a temptation to spend frivolously. You might move to a bigger house thus increasing your rent, you lease a better car, you eat out more often, and before you know it, your new budget has absorbed any increase in income you might have attained. If we are mindful of this and keep our spending consistent, over time hopefully your income rises, and you should be committing, as a percentage, less of your salary towards needs and more towards saving. So, for example, as you earn more, you may spend only 20% on needs, 50% on wants and 30% on savings – a 20/50/30 budget.

This type of budgeting is meant to be aspirational. You are always driving towards getting that saving percentage higher and the other two percentages lower. For many, this will represent the first time you have taken an in-depth look at your spending habits. It also teaches us two very important lessons about how we view money.

The first and most important lesson learnt from this budget is it helps us define the difference between needs and wants. The truth, if we are honest with ourselves, is that even if you consider yourself careful with your money, you will quickly see that there is significant room for savings in your monthly budget.

What you consider a need, upon closer examination, may be a want. For example, a holiday abroad to a sunny location may on the surface have huge benefits to improving your mood and making you happy, so could be perceived as a need, but when compared with a low-cost holiday to a local location, many of the same benefits can be realised.

You won't get that photo on a beach that you can share with your followers on Instagram, but guess what, many of your friends who are posting similar pics are doing so by ignoring their financial future. If we can overcome the need to impress others by spending money more on our needs and less on our wants and building a savings habit, we will dramatically change our financial future.

If we think about other wants that we often perceive as needs, they could include home internet access. Can you use your phone? Cable television with all the sport? How much-added benefit do you truly get from this over a free package? A big house? Again, nothing shows those around you that you're a big shot like having a big house, but these can be expensive to run, and unless house prices are skyrocketing which, if viewed alongside other investments over the last 100 years, they are not, then your money is better placed elsewhere. Same goes for the new car, the latest phone, the best clothes or the best restaurants. In 2016 UK households spent more than £45 a week on average at restaurants and hotels. Is this necessary?

All of these are generally purchased to make ourselves feel superior and show others how successful we are. If we can get away from the need to prove this and out of a mindset of needing others' approval and validation, we are more likely to get on the road to wealth.

In the end, proportional budgeting is useful both from a financial and psychological perspective as it shows you how you're using your money and for what purpose. As you begin analysing your spending, you can begin analysing your day-to-day choices and what is motivating you to make them.

Keep on Top of Your Regular Bills

Stanley Kirk Burrell was born on March 30, 1963, in Oakland, California. Oakland is known as having one of the highest crime rates in the USA with large amounts of urban poverty driven by an escalating drug problem. Burrell's father was a professional poker player and gambling casino manager. However, he was not a prominent figure in Burrell's life who grew up poor with his mother and eight siblings in a small apartment in East Oakland.

Burrell's early recollections were of six children crammed into a three-bedroom housing project apartment.

To make ends meet, Burrell would sell stray baseballs in the car park of the local baseball stadium. He would also indulge his other passion of dancing to a beatbox, often to large crowds.

It was whilst dancing in the car park that Oakland A's team owner Charles O. Finley saw the 11-year-old doing splits and, noticing his obvious energy and flair, hired him as a batboy and office assistant – a role he kept between 1973 and 1980.

You and I know Burrell as MC Hammer. Hammer went on to release 12 albums in his music career. When he hit our screens in baggy trousers and released his hit album 'Please Hammer Don't Hurt 'Em' in 1990, Forbes estimated his income at $33 million that year.

Not long after, in 1996, according to Business Insider, Hammer filed for bankruptcy protection with a total of $1 million in assets and at least $10 million in debts. Years later, Hammer told Oprah Winfrey his debt wasn›t a result of frivolous spending. He said, 'I took my money and employed 200 people in my community. I had a payroll of a million dollars a month at times'.

Hammer had made a mistake that many of us make, albeit on a much larger scale, he didn't monitor and track his monthly bills and as a result they ended up swallowing a vast amount of money.

It is unlikely that if you are reading this, you have a large entourage of people where cutting their salaries is going to help you balance the books. However, it is highly likely you have several fixed monthly outgoings that could be optimised.

Typically, most people are paying:

- Gas and electricity bills
- TV, broadband and phone bills
- Water bills
- Contents insurance
- Council tax
- Mortgage repayments
- TV licence service charges
- Ground rent in flats
- Transport costs
- Food

For some of these bills, where they relate to tax or legal requirements, there is very little you can do to reduce them; however, for many of them, there are large savings that can be made.

The way you save money on each of these bills is simple. You compare them with other providers on a regular basis and then switch to the cheapest. If you haven't used a price comparison site before, there is a handy guide on the money advice service website: https://www.moneyadvice-eservice.org.uk/en/articles/price-comparison-sites-guide

Simply put, the companies who provide the services you pay monthly for do not reward loyalty. In fact, they punish it. The longer you stay with, for example, an energy provider, the more you can expect to be paying over the prevailing market rate and there is no such thing a bad electricity!

The good news is it has never been easier to track when better deals are available. Companies such as moneysavingexpert.com, comparethemarket.com and Uswitch all have automated services that will notify you when a cheaper energy deal is available. You can then switch usually in a few minutes with little effort or admin required.

For the worst offenders, I am going to break down how much can be saved each month using data from price comparison websites and then show how much this could be worth if you invested this money for 30 years in stocks and shares (assuming a 6% annual return).

Bill type	Average monthly saving	Value if invested for 30 years at 6%
Gas and electricity bills	£20 (money supermarket)	£20,090.30
Broadband	£10 (Which?)	£10,045.15
Mobile phone	£16.25 (Oxford University)	£16,323.37

Car insurance	£29.08 (comparet he market.com)	£29,211.30
Total	£75.33	£75,670.33

The total savings from just comparing these four bills and then investing them is an increase in wealth of £77,000 in the long term. In the UK this would double the amount people have saved for retirement. Looking at it another way, this is how much money people are wasting simply by not spending a bit of time every year to review what they are paying.

Where Else Can We Save Each Month?

Regular bills are just one area of your finances that can be improved. Once you get into the habit of looking for bargains, you will quickly see opportunities everywhere in your life where you can streamline your spending and find other improvements (of 1% or more).

Online Purchases

Laszlo Hanyecz is a Florida-based programmer working for online retail company GoRuck. He has a rather unfortunate claim to fame. Hanyecz is a Bitcoin legend and credited with one of the first ever exchanges of Bitcoin for a physical product.

Back in May 2010, he offered 10,000 Bitcoins for two pizzas from Papa John's. Jeremy Sturdivant, also known by his handle Jercos, was on the other side of this trade and delivered the pizzas to Laszlo. At the time Bitcoin didn't have any real-world value; however, at its peak, Lazlo effectively paid about $190 million for those two pizzas. Ouch…

This chapter is about making sure you get a good deal whenever you are shopping. Let's take an example.

It's Friday night, and you have decided to have a relaxed evening and are sitting in front of the TV when you get a little hungry. Being the tech-savvy individual that you are, you whip out your smartphone and search for a takeaway from your local Pizza delivery service. You order, and whilst you wait you realise that you're running low on washing detergent so open your Amazon Prime service and order a pack of it to be delivered the following day. Job done, Pizza arrives, Netflix, chill.

Now let's rewind and see how, with a few minutes of effort, you could have saved on your evening's purchases.

Firstly, pizza delivery. There are a huge number of discount sites that will give you additional money off your food delivery, and they are free, often don't even require you to sign up and are very quick to use. In the UK, vouchercodes.co.uk at the time of writing had over 100 deals for Pizza's, many of which you could use in addition to the discounts that you get from the Pizza company already. These can range from 25% to up to 50% off the purchase price. For the Friday night Pizza enthusiast, these savings add up over time.

Amazon has everything a busy shopper needs, but it is essential that if you are going to use this fast and efficient service, you make the most of the deals that are available to you.

You can reduce your Amazon bill with these three tips:

- Look for Amazon prepaid cards. If you work for a large employer, you might find they have discount cards for large retailers. By charging an Amazon discount card, you can often save around 5% on any money you spend on this site.

- In the example, we used, as it was a regular purchase you can use Amazon's Subscribe and Save service. With the click of a button, you can order and manage your repeat purchases and receive up to 15% off those costly necessities.
- When you buy from Amazon, you can also have a large impact on the price you pay. You can expect significant savings during Prime Week and Cyber Week near Christmas time.
- Delete the Amazon app. Logging into Amazon creates that extra step that can act as a barrier against impulse spending.

According to research by PRRI 48% of millennials, 39% of Generation Xers and 32% of baby boomers used online coupons in 2016. Given that most major retailers will offer money off through vouchers or prepaid cards there is a huge amount that could potentially be saved.

For example, food retailer Sainsbury's will give you up to 8% off everything you spend if you put money on a prepaid Sainsbury's charge card. Beware, companies do this as people often lose their cards or don't spend all the money on the card, so the retailer on average makes more money despite this saving. As long as you aren't one of these people, they are extremely useful and can help you hit your spending targets in your budget.

The lesson here is before you make any purchase online, take the time to compare prices using sites such as PriceGrabber or automate the process using browser add-ons to be alerted when a product you're viewing online is cheaper at another site. Then, check for coupon codes from sites such as Vouchercodes.co.uk, RetailMeNot and Rather-Be-Shopping to get a discount when you checkout.

Recently, I was looking to buy a new dryer for our house, and given the cost, I felt I needed to go the extra mile to make sure I didn't pay top dollar.

After doing my research on comparison websites to find out which product offered the best quality for the most reasonable price, it was then time to find who was willing to give me the best deal.

By simply googling the product, in this case, Hotpoint FETV60CP, you can quickly see that there is a lot of money to be made or lost by not shopping around.

In the case of my dryer, there was a difference of £65.02 between the highest and lowest price. The lowest price also comes with an additional £15 off the order if you sign up to a £1 subscription with one of the site's partners that can be cancelled whenever you wish.

A small saving but given the amount spent online each year, this can add up. In the UK, according to the Office of National Statistics, the average household spends roughly £83.50 a week on household goods and service. It is not unrealistic to assume that by adopting these , we could easily save £20 per month on what we spend, which, if invested for 30 years, adds up to another £20,090.30.

> Hotpoint First Edition FETV 60C P Front-Loading Electric Dryer
> 4.7 ★★★★★ 534 user reviews
>
> Shop now   Sponsored
>
> £219.00 · John Lewis   By Google
>
> £164.97 · Appliances Direct   By Google
> Energy: C
>
> £219.00 · AO.com   By Google
> Energy: C
>
> £204.00 · Boots Kitchen Appliances   By Google
> Energy: C
>
> £178.00 · Electrical Discount UK   By Crowdstorm
> Energy: C
>
> £199.00 · Co-op Electrical Shop   By Google
>
> £199.00 · Robert Dyas   By Google
>
> £219.00 · Marks Electrical   By Kelkoo
> Energy: C
>
> £229.00 · Tesco Direct   By Google
>
> £229.99 · Very   By Google
>
> Product details
>
> Brand: Hotpoint
> Power source: Electric
> Capacity: 6 Kilogram Capacity
> Energy Class: Class C
> Standard Drying Programme: Cotton
> Weighted Drying Programme Time: 82 min

Eating Out for Lunch

In 2017 there were around 250 working days minus your holiday allowance. That means that unless there is some function going on in the office or you work for a trendy start-up where your food is provided for free, you will have to eat lunch at work around 250 times per year.

That is 250 times a year where you can either spend over the odds or save money. For example, in the UK a cluster of 25 grapes from coffee chain Pret a Manger will cost roughly £1.50 for 165g. Alternatively, you could spend an additional 50p at a supermarket and get grapes to last you the entire week. Similarly, buy two cups of coffee from your local coffee shop, and this could set you back as much as £5.00 whereas a bag of decent filter coffee from the supermarket which costs a similar price will last you 30 cups or more.

I know this is boring and feels a lot like penny-pinching and guess what you're right! The mindset you need to adopt is one where every penny saved can be invested to get you closer to that longer-term goal of financial freedom. Try and make this process fun by appreciating the wins you make through savings and keep track (via a chart or spreadsheet) to show how strong the spending and investing side of your Money Triangle is and therefore how close you are to financial freedom and the chance to work when you wish. Think back to our story from Dave Brailsford and his marginal gains principle. Small, often overlooked improvements are the difference between large long-term positive or negative outcomes for our money.

Small positive daily actions do add up. Research conducted by vouchercloud.com suggests that simply by being organised and budgeting your 250 working lunches per year could save you £5 per meal. A small change in your lunchtime habits can really add up. A saving of this amount could add up to £108 per month which if invested at a 6% return for 30 years gives you a total of £108,487.62. All from just being mindful about buying lunch.

In this section we have only tackled the working lunch; however, there are many areas of our eating habits we could target. The Bureau of Labour Statistics found that the average person spends more than £2,300 a year on meals out at restaurants. A 50% decrease on this spend could save us another £100 per month or, if invested, this could be worth £100,451.50 in 30 years.

Yes, it's boring; yes, your friends will think you're weird bringing your lunch in whilst they take photos for their Instagram profile of their £15 vegan salad bowl, but it really will add up in the long run. If you needed another excuse, research by the Dietitians Association of Australia has also shown that those who bring in their lunch, eat fewer calories and are generally healthier with more energy, so if you care, take photos of those new washboard abs instead (http://www.huffingtonpost.com.au/2016/04/12/bringing-lunch-to-work_n_9675486.html).

Drinking and Going Out

We have all woken up after a heavy night out with a massive hangover and an empty wallet. Regret usually quickly sets in as we realise we are likely to have to scrimp and save for the rest of the month.

Perhaps unsurprisingly, our age tends to correlate with how much we spend going out. Millennials go out to eat more often than Gen X or baby boomers, according to Morgan Stanley analysts. Fifty-three per cent of millennials go out to eat once a week, compared with 43% for the general population. Interestingly, although millennials are going out more often, they are increasingly drinking less, and we are seeing the rise of the sober socialite. However, if, like me, you are guilty of going out and drinking with friends a little too often, this section is for you.

Cait Flanders, a contributor to the Huffington Post, is in a similar boat to many of us. She drank too much growing up, and things seemed to only get worse as she got older and entered the working world. A year ago, she decided to go cold turkey and run the numbers to see what the true cost of alcohol had been throughout her life.

She started her drinking career, as many of us do, drinking cheap cider and spirits. She estimates this cost her between $7 and $12 per week and given that she started very young; by the time she left school, she estimates she had spent $2,340 on alcohol.

At this point, Cait went to college where drinking and partying became much more of a focus. She would usually go out between two and three times per week and could spend anything from $40 to $80 a week. In total, over her 4 years at University, she spent $12,440.

It is at this point that things took a slightly darker turn for Cait:

'If I'm being honest, the next few years are a bit of a blur — not that I don't remember them, but there's a lot I've chosen to forget about. For the first year, I was in an extremely toxic relationship. We lived together, so I wasn't out at the bar every weekend with my girlfriends, but we still partied a lot. Some weeks, we'd be good and stay at home – maybe have a few friends over for drinks. Other weeks, I'd easily drop $100 on a night out. We also drank a lot when we went away, and I have no idea how much I spent then. I'll lowball and say it was still $60/week for the year we were together.

After we broke up, I binged – on both drinking and spending. I tried to buy a new life. I moved into a one-bedroom apartment by myself and filled it with brand new furniture (that I put on credit). I also financed a brand new car. I thought that if things looked like they were pieced together, that's how I would feel. Of course, it didn't work.

Living alone also gave me the freedom to drink as much as I wanted without anyone watching over me. I had friends over every weekend, and we'd split a few bottles of wine or packs of Strongbow, before heading downtown for the night. It was common for me to start a tab at a club and tell my friends to put all their drinks on it because I wanted to make sure the party never ended.

I can't say for sure how much money I spent on partying during the two years I lived alone because this was when I started racking up my credit card debt, ignoring my statements and making only the minimum payments. I know there were nights where I'd drink nothing more than a $10 bottle of wine at home, but there were also nights where I'd say to my server, 'whenever my wine glass is empty, that means I want another'. On those nights, I do remember that my bill was typically in the $80–120 range and that rarely included food. I'm lowballing again, but let's say I spent $100/week on partying then.

Drinking and spending to fill an emotional void are incredibly common, and both habits will destroy your finances. In Cait's case, she estimates she has spent $35,712 on partying; that's $2,463/year for 14.5 years (https://www.huffingtonpost.com/cait-flanders/the-true-cost-of-wasting-money-on-getting-wasted_b_9721960.html).

I don't advocate sitting at home being bored and not socialising. It is a quick way to lose friends and your mind. What we need to look at is how we optimise this weekly spend and improve it by a small amount. Let's not go overboard but keep the 1% principle in mind. Even two fewer drinks a week could save you anywhere between £5 and £15 depending on where you are buying them. It is not unreasonable to say that for a socially active person, there is probably £30 a month that you could save just by skipping a couple of drinks each time you go out. If instead of spending it you invested it for the long term, this could be worth £52,327.78 in 30 years' time. Plus, it may also save you a hangover or two.

Smoking

I have left this one until last. If you aren't a smoker, smart decision, you can skip this section.

You've heard it a million times: Smoking is bad for you, but if the warnings that smoking can lead to lung disease and cancer haven't convinced you to quit, maybe the high cost of your habit will.

The price of a pack of 20 cigarettes is £12.55. If you have a three pack a week habit, you are spending somewhere in the region of £150 a month. This saving invested monthly for 30 years would be worth £261,638.11. That is an insane amount of money and the difference between having financial freedom and working until the day you die. In the UK, smoking-related diseases cost the NHS £5 billion a year. That is £5 billion that is not being spent on desperately understaffed hospitals and lifesaving drugs.

If the prospect of cancer, premature death, causing pain to your loved ones and wasting money aren't enough to change your mind, then I'm pretty confident nothing I tell you in this book is going to change anything else in your life so send it back to me for a refund!

Mobile Phones

According to global research by B2X, a provider of customer care for smart mobile and Internet of Things (IoT) devices, nearly 10% of global consumers plan to spend more than $750 on their next smartphone. The same research showed that the amount we spend on personal tech is increasing every year.

I understand in today's society your phone is not just an accessory to show off but essential for everyday living: acting as a wallet, calendar, camera and a million other things. Where the problem begins is not necessarily the phone itself but the mechanism by which we purchase it.

Most people will buy a new phone as part of a new monthly payment plan. Usually, the deal looks something like pay £X per month for a minimum of 2 years and get the latest phone for just £1. Effectively, the £30 per month or £720 throughout 2 years covers the cost of your data and calls, and the rest is used to pay off the cost of the phone. You have entered into a finance agreement with the phone company. It is difficult to work out the sort of interest rate you are charged, but it is usually a double-digit percentage albeit hidden behind some very clever marketing.

Although many mobile phone contracts combine the cost of the plan and handset over a certain length of time, the costs are not always split. This means that even when you have finished paying off the phone after your 2-year fixed period, your monthly fee will not go down unless you either move the contract or call up your provider and tell them you are thinking of leaving.

This practice is extremely common, and in the UK, consumers are collectively losing out on £355 million a year on handsets they have bought already but continue to pay for via their bill.

It is essential that we monitor when our phone contracts expire and ensure you jump on your carrier to renegotiate your deal.

Making Impulse Purchases

#worstimpulsebuy gives you some very amusing results if you have a quick search on Twitter. Items include Halloween ghost dog costumes, electric vegetable peelers and paintball gear that never gets used. Not forgetting a Louis Vuitton bag, bought on vacation, that sits in a closet talking to other impulse buys.

Advertisers love impulse buyers. Retailers spend millions every year looking at behavioural psychology and nudges to get us in the mood to purchase when otherwise we would not do so.

A recent Forbes article tackling the subject of impulse buying highlighted studies that have shown that impulsive shopping is incited by both internal and external factors: internally, we perceive impulsive shopping as adventurous, exciting and even a means of escape. On the external side, retailers play with promotional pressure ('get 50% off for *a limited time only!*'), enticing displays strategically placed by the cash registers, and even price-anchoring games that give items an inflated list-price and a hefty discount in order to trick the consumer into thinking they›re getting a phenomenal deal. All these tactics are designed to get us reaching for our wallets (https://www.forbes.com/sites/maggiemcgrath/2015/10/25/shameful-shopping-secrets-revealed-twitter-users-recount-their-worst-impulse-purchases/#a79737d41dae).

A CreditCards.com survey published in 2016 found that five out of six Americans have made impulse purchases. Some can be quite expensive: 25% said they spent $500 or more, and 17% said they spent $1,000 or more on impulse buys. In our world of scraping together marginal gains to hit long-term financial independence, this area is ripe for improvement (https://www.creditcards.com/credit-card-news/impulse-buy-survey.php).

What the research also tells us is that we all have triggers that cause us to buy impulsively. In other words, on any given day, we might be more likely to buy something impulsively than on another day. CreditCards.com found that men are more likely to make impulse purchases when intoxicated, and women tend to do it when they're sad. Being aware of when you might be more vulnerable is a great first step towards stopping action that is sabotaging your wealth creation. The next time you find your head turned by a specific bargain or headline in a shop window or website, try taking a moment to reflect and take stock of your mood.

The website becomingminimalist.com provides you with three questions you should ask yourself before any purchase. Let's take buying clothes. You should ask yourself:

1. Am I replacing an item of clothing or buying something new? If the item is not a specific replacement, rethink your need for it.

2. Is this something I will wear regularly? If you can't see yourself wearing the item regularly, rethink the purchase.
3. Is the style one that will last? Don't believe all the hype of the latest trends as they are manufactured by the fashion industry to drive regular purchases and change quickly.

For more questions around what should be asked when buying everything from technology to food, check out the becomingminimalist.com for some great tips.

One trick that you might want to try when shopping online if you are not in a hurry is the abandoned cart strategy.

Online retailers are painfully aware that customers are getting to the checkout and then leaving just before they make their purchase, costing them serious money. The current rate of abandonment online at the point of checkout is almost 70% (https://baymard.com/lists/cart-abandonment-rate). For this reason, it makes a lot of sense for these retailers to try and tempt you back and complete your purchase because, after all, you were so close! This can also prove far cheaper for retailers than chasing new customers.

Although this is unlikely to work with the likes of Amazon, if you go to smaller retailers, once you have registered with an email address, go to the checkout with your purchase and then exit the process at the point where you would normally pay.

If the site is going to give you a discount for an abandoned cart, then you will usually know within 24 hours. These can vary massively but, in my experience, can be up to

20% off and will take the form of a discount code. Abandoning your cart will also allow you to think about whether you really need the product and it is amazing how, after 24 hours, you find you didn't really need to buy it in the first place.

The idea is to adopt a mindset of conscious consumption whereby you are only buying products and services that serve a specific need and purpose – giving you more personal value than the price paid. This will have the effect to not only save you money but declutter your life.

Behavioural Changes

Its payday and you check your bank account. Boom, your pay has cleared, and your account is looking good! The first thought that comes to mind is you have to pay off all pending utility, credit card and phone bills as well as that annoying rent or mortgage payment. That out of the way and still feeling flush, you remember those new shoes that you saw in the shop last week when you had no money in your account, and you go out and buy them. The first Friday after payday hits, so you call your friends to meet them for dinner and then hit the town. You go to that new club, buy a bottle of something expensive for the table, snap a few selfies and upload them to Instagram #YOLO.

The following day you wake up with a hangover, take a look at your bank account and realise that you have little if anything left to live on for the rest of the month, let alone put some away to save for the future.

This boom and bust sequence of spending is the quickest way to ensure that you never build up any financial resilience and live payday to payday.

How Do We Combat This?

You can't spend what you don't have. The easiest way to stop spending unnecessarily is to positively sabotage yourself to take away the ability to overspend.

Your first step is to work out your essential expenditure also known as your 'needs' category from the previous chapter. You then need to work out what your take-home pay is and take off your essential expenditure from this figure. This is your monthly cash buffer.

The larger your monthly cash buffer, the more options you have and the easier it is to create long-term wealth. You can increase your monthly cash buffer by either spending less on needs or earning more. If you are finding that you have very little left over despite not spending anything on your 'wants', don't fret; we will tackle additional earning strategies in our 'How to Earn It' section.

Let's rewind to the start of the month. Now, as your money hits your account, two things will happen.

You decided to adopt the 70/15/15 budget from the previous chapter; therefore, the amount of money that comes from your employer will already have been reduced as you have ensured some of it has been paid into your long-term savings account – a pension or similar savings vehicle. This usually has the advantage that you get any income tax that would usually be paid back so could mean an instant return on the money of between 20% and 40%, depending on your tax rate. Employers are also often willing to match your contribution up to a certain percentage of your salary, meaning, alongside the tax rebate, you can often more than double the money you save with no extra effort. If you claim the additional employer match, you have also just boosted your salary.

Secondly, you set up a separate savings account. When your salary hits your main account, ensure there is an automated direct debit that transfers a percentage of your salary to your savings account. Start small but aim to increase this over time. For example, if you get a pay rise, aim to put a minimum of half of it into your savings account.

This savings account aims to build up your financial resilience. Financial resilience is your ability to survive a financial shock such as losing your job, the boiler exploding or your car breaking down. Once you have 3 months' worth of your salary saved into this account, you have your emergency cash buffer. This money should be sitting in an account that is risk free with the best interest rate you can find. If you need to raid it in times of emergency, then the following month you need to begin topping it up as a priority.

Once you have your emergency fund built up, it is time to open a third savings account. This is your medium-term savings account and will need to be opened somewhere that gives you access to investments that can provide real investment returns for you such as stocks and shares.

With these two actions in place and automated every month without lifting a finger, you will begin to improve your financial resilience. You are paying yourself first not after all other expenses have been paid. Your spending on your 'wants' only occurs after you have spent on your 'savings'.

The main downside to this strategy is that you will have less in your main account to live on. Many of the experts in the research that was done for this book suggested that having a separate allocation of your cash buffer for spending on luxuries was a good way to make sure this didn't get out of control. If you set aside a specific amount each month for this purpose, you will be more inclined to spend mindfully.

We all need to live and find a comfortable place on the Money-Life Balance, but if you are drowning in debt and have no cash in the bank at the end of each month, your spending side of the Money Triangle will never be strong. In this situation, I am an advocate for radical action. There is no way of sugar coating it; you're going to have to stop going out and pull back on all luxuries. It's not forever. Only until you can breathe a little more easily and are no longer living month to month.

Mismanaging Debt

Hi all,

I am a first time poster, would appreciate if I could get some help from you all. Before I start, I would like to confirm that I am indeed an idiot for getting myself into this situation and take full responsibility for it.

The situation I am in is quite dire, I have Payday loans with several companies, total amounting to around £5000.00. Here is a breakdown below:

Satsuma (total owed £900.00) - payments of £28.50 per week

QuickQuid (total owed £1695.00) - first payment is for £198.00

PoundsToPocket (total owed £1750.00) - £150.00 per month

Sunny (total owed £460.00) - £460.00 due end of month

MyJar (total owed £114.00) - £114.00 due next week

Lending Stream (total owed £115.00) - £38.50 due end of month

Wage Day Advance (total owed £180.00) - £180.00 due end of month

Payday Loans UK/memecredit (total owed £440.00) - £440.00 due end of month

I am penniless until 29th of January, and am in fact already over my planned overdraft by £350.00 (so when my wage comes in, it will deduct £350.00 from my overdraft automatically). I have two bank accounts, one where my salary goes into and one which PDL [Pay Day Loan] companies pay into, so in that sense I am in control of what happens when I get paid.

I live with family and voluntarily pay £200.00 in rent (family do not know about my debt crisis and ideally I would like to keep it away from them...). I could probably live off £350-400 a month (incl. voluntary rent) which leaves my disposable income to £1400 a month to pay these lenders.

If I get things right, I am slightly optimistic that I can get things at least under control after two paydays, but I need your help to prioritise which of these loans should I pay first and which should I try to negotiate a repayment plan with? This month it is impossible for me to pay all my lenders.

Also, because I will be over my planned overdraft by £350 (will be charged £10/day) what should I tell my bank? What will the immediate consequences be?

I know I made a stupid decision, I am only 22, and find myself in such a situation whilst most people my age are saving up etc. it is very depressing but I want to sort things out now...

Appreciate all replies,

Thanks.

edit: just a quick summary, disposable income for this month will be around £1300. Total owed this month is £1609 in PDL alone.

The above story appeared on the Money Saving Expert website community board and was caused by a gambling addiction. This shows how mismanaging your money and turning to high-priced debt can have a huge impact both financially and mentally. This can happen to anyone so it makes a lot of sense to understand what debt is and how to avoid the bad types of debt that can come back and bite us.

Bad debts, to put it simply, are those that drain your wealth. They tend to be unaffordable and offer no real prospect of 'paying for themselves' in the future. Put another way, bad debts are used to buy things that don't provide any income and are likely to decrease in value over time.

Bad debts likely have no real time frame or plan regarding how you are going to pay them off. They tend to have very high interest rates and are often used to make large impulse purchases of products that people don't need. You might also find bad debt creeping into your life if you are spending too much on the day to day and need to borrow to cover everyday essentials such as bills. As a general rule of thumb, if you can't afford to borrow the money (e.g. you aren't sure you'll be able to make the monthly repayments), it is definitely a bad debt.

Some examples of items that are often bought using borrowed money and classify as bad debt include:

- **New technology:** unless this is essential to achieving a job or task, there is often very little reason to upgrade your phone or laptop. Once purchased, this tech is highly likely to rapidly decrease in value so you will definitely lose money if you ever wished to resell it.

- **A store card for luxury clothes:** generally, these cards have extortionate borrowing rates where you can pay multiples of what you borrow and likely for stuff that will be out of fashion in months or even days.

- **A luxury holiday you can't afford:** a luxury holiday is an amazing experience and one you are unlikely to forget, but best avoided if accompanied by a lifetime of debt. The best way to enjoy a luxury holiday is to make allowances in your budget and build up a savings pot from which you can buy the holiday; for example, saving £100 per month could give you a budget of £1,200 for holidays each year, and this doesn't include any potential investment growth that amount could achieve.

- **A brand-new car you don't need:** a new car will lose roughly 20% of its value the moment you drive it out of the showroom. If it isn't essential, then you don't need it. If it's something you have to buy, and you are looking at buying it on finance, be mindful of the cost of the debt as you can often find a better value loan away from the dealer's finance schemes.

- **Borrowing money to pay bills and or other credit:** there are several free financial advice services in most countries that can help you analyse your spending and give you advice if the debt is ever becoming a serious concern. If you find yourself borrowing to cover day-to-day essential expenditure, then you need to take serious action to decrease your outgoings.

You may have identified similarities from the list above from our previous chapter on budgeting. Bad debts are often those that are used to satisfy our wants, so always ask yourself which category your purchase falls into before reaching for the credit card or going online to look for a loan.

What Is Good Debt?

In simple terms, the opposite of bad debt!

Good debt is one that is used to fund a sensible investment in your financial future. Although it is perhaps speculative at times, the aim of the debt is that it should leave you better off in the long term and should not harm your overall financial position.

Good debts tend to have detailed and competitive payment terms. You will have a clear and specific reason for taking it out, and a realistic plan for paying it back that allows you to clear the debt as quickly as possible, or in a series of regular and affordable payments (e.g. for a mortgage).

The financial decision is thought through, and often you will have compared several different lenders and solutions to work out which one is best for you.

To find the best solution, you will have found an interest rate that is the lowest available, borrowed only as much as you absolutely need and attained the best payment terms and period to pay it off.

Not being clued up about debt can lead to serious misery. Borrowing rates can be vary from 0% to as high at 5,000%, meaning you end up paying back 50 times what you borrow if you don't pay off the loan within a year. Regulations are catching up to this sort of predatory lending, but it still pays to have your wits about you.

We can't talk about debt without also talking about mortgages.

According to new data from Apartment List, 80% of millennials have the desire to buy their own home (https://www.apartmentlist.com/rentonomics/american-dream-home-ownership-delayed-millennial-generation/).

This is hardly surprising as in many countries around the world property is regularly cited as the way to get rich. Booming populations and lack of supply have often meant that there have been huge increases in property prices. These have been appealing to investors looking to get rich as you can often only put down a small amount of money to buy a property and borrow the rest. If the property then increases in value, you can multiply your initial investment (as a result of leverage). We must be very careful as this can have the opposite effect if property prices go down and our loses can skyrocket. Whether for investment or to own your own home, it is worth knowing about mortgages so you can avoid many of the common pitfalls.

Mortgages can be confusing with a lot of different terms that you need to get your head around to understand whether the mortgage you are looking at is offering you good value for money.

What Is a Mortgage?

A mortgage is a loan that you take out that allows you to purchase your property. In return for lending you the money, the bank expects you to pay them back the full amount borrowed plus interest. The bank will also have the right to sell your home and recoup the loan if you don't keep up with your payments.

Let's use Jill as an example. Jill decides to buy a house and needs to borrow £200,000. Her bank offers her an interest rate of 3%. Her bank will charge her this interest monthly. Three per cent per year divided by 12, the number of months in the year, is roughly 0.25% per month. Multiply 0.25% by £200,000, and you get £416.66 as the monthly interest payment.

If you have what is known as an interest-only mortgage, then that is all you will have to pay each month; however, at the end of the loan period, you will still owe the original £200,000.

If you have a repayment mortgage, then each month you will pay the interest plus some money towards paying off the balance of the loan to ensure after the loan period is over there is no balance left.

If Jill had chosen to borrow the £200,000 over 25 years on a full repayment basis, then her total monthly payment would be £948. You can see the table below which shows how the debt is gradually paid off over time.

Year	Remaining debt
0	£200,000
1	£194,543
2	£188,920
3	£183,127
4	£177,157
5	£171,006
6	£164,668
7	£158,137
8	£151,407
9	£144,473
10	£137,328
11	£129,966
12	£122,380
13	£114,564
14	£106,510
15	£98,211
16	£89,660
17	£80,849
18	£71,770
19	£62,415
20	£52,775
21	£42,843
22	£32,608
23	£22,063
24	£11,197
25	£0

Although the monthly figure that you pay doesn't change, in the first few years of the mortgage, you're paying proportionally more interest, so the debt only reduces slowly, as the table above shows. Over time the payments begin to eat into the capital sum. You can massively reduce the overall amount that you pay back by making overpayments which can eat into the debt and reduce the amount of interest you pay; however, you should always check there aren't overpayment penalties beforehand.

Fixed Versus Variable Interest Rates

The amount of interest you pay on a mortgage is worked out by the interest rate that you agree to when you sign up to the mortgage. A mortgage on which the interest rate is set for the life of the loan is called a 'fixed-rate mortgage'. In this example, you will only pay one rate regardless of movements in the interest rate. These will benefit you if interest rates go up over time and you have locked in a lower rate.

A variable rate mortgage will fluctuate with the interest rate of the country that you are borrowing in. For example, if you live in the UK and the Bank of England puts up rates, then you would expect your monthly payments to increase. These mortgages will be better if interest rates are going down over time, so you are not locking in a higher rate.

In practice, most mortgages will have a fixed and variable rate element to them. For example, you might sign up to a special initial rate where you get the first two years of the mortgage as a fixed low-interest rate before it then switches to a variable mortgage. You would then have the opportunity to switch your provider to take advantage of better deals. For many people this could result in significant monthly savings and reduce the cost of your essential monthly spending.

Credit Rating

JB had always held an excellent credit rating and obtaining 0% interest credit cards had never been a problem, until recently. About 3 years ago, he signed up for the Amazon credit card. He used it for about a year and then, with the balance clear, cut up the card, but unfortunately didn't close the account.

He then moved across the country from Manchester to Cornwall. At his new house he purchased an album from the Amazon MP3 store for £7.99. At the payment screen, he didn't check the default credit card (which turned out to be the Amazon card) and continued on his way.

Seven months later he asked his mortgage company for further borrowing to do some home improvements. This loan was accepted, but they advised he should check out his credit score as there appeared to be a problem.

He signed up to Experian and found that he had missed six months' payments on the Amazon credit card. He immediately called the company and cleared the debt along with £25 late charges and thought that was the end of it. The company stated they had been sending reminder letters to his previous address. He explained he had moved and it was a silly mistake.

Since then he has not been able to get credit. He was advised to add a reason to his credit report, explaining the problem, but this appears to have had no effect. He has written to Amazon Credit Card Services twice and they have refused to change the notes on his report, and, as a final attempt, he wrote to the Financial Ombudsmen, but as yet have has not had a reply.

He has never been bankrupted, has no other financial red marks against his name, earns over £60,000 per year and has a mortgage for only 50% of his property. He recently inquired into a car leasing as he is about to transfer from a company car scheme to a cash for car scheme, but this was refused. It's a dire situation, especially when the root of the problem is a silly mistake worth £25.

The above story was written to Guardian newspaper's financial expert Miles Brignall and highlights how important it is that we understand what our credit rating is.

A credit rating is simply an estimate of your ability to pay back money that you borrow. The higher your credit score, the more lenders will be willing to give to you and the lower the interest rates will be.

If you are looking to borrow money, then it makes sense to do everything you can to improve this score so you get the lowest interest rates which will save you considerable amounts of money in the long term.

Several companies provide free apps and services aimed at helping you improve your credit score. These include Equifax, ClearScore, Experian and many others. They will provide training and tips to help you improve your credit rating and improve your chances of being offered a loan. These apps will also highlight the best deals that are currently available for customers with your profile looking for credit cards, short-term loans and mortgages.

Your credit score is made up of loads of different data points, and ensuring none of these is flashing red will make a big difference to your score. To make sure your credit score is going in the right direction, you should consider the following factors:

1. Payment history: if you have borrowed money in the past, did you pay it back on time? Payment history, along with public records (see below), generally accounts for approximately 35% of your score. A record of late payments on your current and past credit accounts will typically lower your score. Being consistent about paying on time can, over time, have a positive impact on your score.

2. Public records: this can have a large impact on your credit score if you have a public record of bankruptcies, judgments and collection items. Be aware of these, even if you can't always avoid them. If you have one, don't fret. Credit scores are fluid and can improve over time so it is still possible for you to have a perfect credit score even after a bankruptcy.

3. Length of credit history: in general, a longer credit history is better and can sometimes have a positive impact on your score. The more reliable you can show you are over a longer period, the better. Credit history typically accounts for around 15% of your score.

4. New accounts: this might seem odd but opening multiple new accounts in a short period may negatively impact your score. Keep your late-night erratic behaviour to a minimum!

5. Inquiries: whenever someone else gets your credit report such as a lender, landlord, or insurer, an inquiry is recorded on your credit report. A large number of recent inquiries may negatively impact your score. Your new credit accounts and inquiries generally make up about 10% of your score. Think about someone who continually runs around asking people if they can borrow money but not necessarily taking it. Wouldn't that make you a little suspicious?

6. Accounts in use: simplifying your financial life will not only make it easier to keep track of but can improve your credit rating. The presence of too many open accounts can hurt your score, whether you're using the accounts or not. This activity usually makes up approximately 10% of your score.

I am aware that when you talk about interest rates and credit scores, a lot of people's eyes will glaze over. Unfortunately, this stuff is important to get your head around if you are looking at borrowing money, which, if you are buying appreciating assets, can massively increase the money you make when it is time to sell.

Where would Brailsford find his 1% in your borrowing behaviour? There are huge savings for those who haven't shopped around for the best credit card deals, mortgages or loans. If you have any borrowing, then you should shop around and look at moving any existing borrowing you have to better rates.

Summary

Many finance and lifestyle commentators really won't like this section as they will see reduction in expenditure as a way of postponing living your life to the full. After all, no one knows what will come tomorrow and you may never get to enjoy those hard-earned savings.

What we spend is an essential part of the Money Triangle, and if you don't have this under control, your money triangle will never be robust and you will never achieve the financial freedom you desire. If in this section you have not found the opportunity to save money particularly motivational, then think of it in terms of time. The average person in the UK, according to ONS data, is earning £30,420 per year or £22,241 after tax. Assuming a normal holiday allowance you will be working 240 days a year which, if you are working 10 hours a day, that means you are earning £9.26 per hour after tax.

I have found that looking at everyday purchases in the context of how long I would have to work in order to pay for them can make a bigger impression on my spending than the amount saved. For example, does a £10 taxi ride (that takes over an hour of work to pay for) actually save you any time if you could walk it? Or is a coffee from Starbucks worth the 20 minutes of your time that it takes to pay for it?

The answers to these questions come from the value that you derive from the purchase. For example, the coffee may not be worth it but the time spent reconnecting with a friend and relaxing outside of the office might make it extremely valuable to you and your friend.

It is not just what you spend but also how you spend that is an essential component of the Money Triangle. Be mindful of where your money is going and only buy what provides you with true value. The legendary investor Warren Buffett put it best with his quote 'Price is what you pay. Value is what you get', so try to ensure every purchase provides you with at least as much value as the price.

How to Earn It

'Lack of money is the root of all evil'.
– George Bernard Shaw

Thais Lage was born in Brazil but at a young age moved with her family to live in Florida. From an early age, she proved herself to be incredibly gifted with numbers and began tutoring struggling students in mathematics from the age of 14. She quickly built up her reputation as a great tutor and was highly sort after by parents in her neighbourhood after they discovered her command of the subject.

Thais was also noticed at school for her obvious ability, and her trigonometry teacher started to introduce her to students who she coached in her spare time. Fairly quickly Thais was earning $100 a week which felt like a lot given her young age.

She kept this entrepreneurial mindset throughout university where she printed flyers and posting them around campus, helping her earn an income to put towards her college tuition. She even tutored her hairstylist in exchange for free haircuts.

In December 2015, Thais graduated with a degree in aerospace engineering and secured her dream job as a Mechanical Systems Engineer at Kennedy Space Centre. As well as being a math tutor, Thais could now claim to be a rocket scientist!

Her job at the Space Centre was demanding but she continued to want to help students who were struggling with their studies, so she continued with her tutoring business despite her gruelling schedule. Her new job as a rocket scientist also gave her a little more prestige and enabled her to increase her hourly rate for some of her customers.

As part of her tutoring service, Thais would often film and email a quick 'how-to' video to her students to help with their homework and they got great feedback. She also noticed that many of the students were struggling with the same problems and she could reuse much of the content.

In September 2018, she started 321 Tutoring with the aim to develop individualised learning plans to help students experience success, confidence, and mathematical agility. She also expanded her service to include adults.

Her start-up costs were only $70 for her website and domain and she also bought an iPad Pro costing around $900. She charges $50/hour for middle-high school mathematics and $80–100/hour for SAT/ACT prep. She recently hired two tutors that work under the 321 Tutoring umbrella, and she keeps 10% of whatever they earn.

The lessons she filmed in the early days of her tutoring are now available on YouTube where she can take a share of advertising revenue for her more popular videos. She plans to hire more tutors to work with her and develop more in-depth online courses that anyone can use to help them develop their math skills. This side hustle generates considerable income that supplements her day job and boosts her take-home pay, allowing her to save more and reach financial freedom sooner.

How to earn it is the second side of the Money Triangle. There are two ways to find the money to invest to create wealth over the long term: spend less or earn more. We have shown in several case studies that even those not earning vast sums of money can accumulate great wealth over the long term by being mindful of what they spend and how they invest it.

Up until this point, we have focused on optimising the money that we currently have. However, the whole journey is made easier if we can radically increase the amount that we are earning and then turbocharge it by applying the lessons learnt in our section on optimising spending. By earning more, we can increase the amount we invest, thus bringing forward the date at which we achieve real financial freedom

You're probably scratching your head now and saying, 'this is all pretty obvious but how do I do it?!'

What we will now dive into is how people have managed to increase their earnings either through their current job, side hustle or even through starting their own business. We will then look at what lessons we can learn from these stories to help ourselves increase our income.

The Working World

In 1993, Chris Rondeau, a student at the University of New Hampshire, had little business experience, other than helping his father manage a chain of New England drug stores. Describing himself as a bit of a 'meathead' and with an interest in health and fitness, he contacted local entrepreneurs Michael and Marc Grondahl who had bought a failing Gold's Gym asking for a job. Spotting Chris's natural charisma, they hired him to run the club's front desk. Chris quickly became the face of the gym. He then moved into personal training and then regional manager roles as the business, renamed Planet Fitness, expanded due to its highly successful low-cost model aimed at the casual gym goer. Chris was always a standout performer at the firm, driving new initiatives and helping the founders manage the explosive growth. He never saw his role as an employee but as a key person within the business responsible for its ongoing growth.

In 2013, after a stint as COO, Chris was named CEO and took the helm of the business seeing his own net worth approach $1 billion as the company's share price skyrocketed.

Chris's example shows that often the easiest way to increase what you earn is to get paid more for what you are currently doing.

In theory, we should all be paid in line with the value we provide to our employer, but it is a sad fact that when valued employees are offered more money to work for a competitor, the firm they currently work for will often look to match it. The question you will often ask yourself in this circumstance is, 'why didn't they just pay me that in the first place?'

This is a tough question to answer as even innovative employers, who highly value their staff, can fall prey to market forces. An organisation will only ever pay you the maximum that they believe you are worth. If they can get you for less than this, then great. This is not to say, however, that other firms might not value your skills more than where you are currently working. This could be due to any number of reasons, but perhaps they are in an environment where they see the skills and experience that you have can generate more value than your current employer. This can often explain why a competitor will offer to pay a lot more than you may currently be receiving even though your employer does regular pay reviews and industry benchmarking.

When these great offers come in for employees of a business, management is left with the decision of whether they wish to retain the person or let them go. They will often have to weigh up several factors, but the most influential tends to be the cost of replacement. Others include:

- If you were to walk out the door, how easily could they find someone of equal or better quality?
- How much would it cost to recruit and train your replacement?
- What is the cost of the disruption to the current business?
- Given the new salary benchmark set by your competitor, would they now not be able to find someone for your old wage to do the same job?

These factors explain why even a highly valued employee can get a great salary offer and then see their current employer match it. It also explains why even if you are highly valued you may get no counter from your current employer.

This might indicate a good strategy is to sit in a job constantly scanning the market for better-paid positions; however, I think we can all agree this is not the way to remain productive. By switching jobs frequently, depending on your role, you can damage your long-term earnings. Yes, you may have found a higher salary, but are they only offering that due to lower staff training budgets, high-pressure cultures and flat management structures with no chance of progression?

What you are paid is a function of the effort you put in and the value you create for the business so expect to struggle to get what you want if you are not a top performer. You must also realise that the amount of money you will be paid in a job will generally be limited if you are not in a position that clearly creates revenue for the business. There is a reason that, outside of founders and CEOs, those who work in sales within an organisation are often the highest paid.

This doesn't mean that you need to quit your job tomorrow and move into a new role. What it does mean is you need to somehow position yourself within your current role to find a way to clearly demonstrate how you add revenue to the business.

Let's take the example of someone who is a manual labourer on a building site. Your role is to come on-site and ensure equipment and materials are where they need to be so skilled labour can install windows, roofs, heating systems, etc. For this role, you are paid a little above minimum wage and probably aren't feeling great about it.

If you were to try and put yourself into a position where you could add revenue to the business, what would you do? One strategy might be to print out a couple of hundred fliers that detail the work that your company can do and then arrive 30 minutes early for work and go door-knocking before you start your shift. You know if you are working on an extension in an affluent street, there are others that are looking out the window wondering if they should do the same. The hit rate is going to be low, but if you got those 200 fliers out to people in the neighbourhood and spoke to them personally, over the course of a month it is not unreasonable to expect that you might be able to get one of them to do business with you. What would your employer pay you for this new work? I would be surprised if it was less than 10% and given the average extension is going to cost no less than £20,000 there is a nice additional income that you can expect for an extra 30 minutes to 1 hour per day.

Timing

Grabbing your boss as they are running into a Board meeting for a quick chat about pay will not get you what you want. Neither will tackling the issue after the company has just announced a record loss. Choose your moment and time it perfectly. If your company seems to be in a spiral of decreasing profits and reducing headcount, then it may be time to question the future of the business and your role within it.

With this in mind, ensure you arrange any remuneration discussions in advance and check with your boss's PA or her diary to ensure there are no other important meetings coming up. You want their undivided attention. Also, don't be afraid to let your boss know why you are calling the meeting so you can both be prepared. You must also be prepared for the meeting. Do you have a clear idea of what you want and how you are going to get it? You need to have a number in mind and push for that. Don't simply say, 'pay me what you think I am worth'. This is a great way to get a low-ball offer or show you aren't taking this conversation seriously enough. State what value you provide to your employer, what you are after and why you feel it is justified. You might want to look at comparable positions in the firm or rival companies. Look at job adverts online and be aware that trade magazines frequently carry out salary surveys.

Talk about your achievements and successes, the value they demonstrate and how you plan to build upon them to create more value for your employer. If possible, get some testimonials from colleagues and, even better, senior members of the company. This is all about building your credibility and value to the business. Testimonials also help to reduce the risk to your boss who might be going out on a limb to give you an inflation-busting pay rise. If she can point to other recommendations, it reduces her risk if things go wrong.

One thing to remember is to also be open-minded. If you choose to work for established organisations you must accept the race up the corporate ladder is a marathon and not a sprint. Pay is only one part of the job package. If you can add to the role you are doing with responsibilities that will pay dividends down the line, then this is also a good outcome and one you should consider. Base salary is also only one option of increasing your take-home pay. You might also consider a change in bonus structure, reduced working hours or increase in other benefits such as pension contributions.

Change Your Behaviour

The best way I have seen to get a pay rise is to start acting and performing like someone who is doing the job you want. This usually involves putting in more effort than is expected of you, such as doing extra work and helping others around you. It might also involve taking on projects that aren't necessarily part of your day job but will provide excellent learning opportunities.

The more indispensable you become and the more problems you solve or revenue you produce for a business, the more likely you are to get a pay rise. Look at what you are doing in your job today. Are you helping your business hit its strategic objectives more than you were a year ago? If not, why would anyone give you a pay rise above the usual rate of inflation? It always amazes me how many people expect to get a massive pay rise without putting in any additional effort. The promise of additional work is not enough. You should always be trying to work at the level of the pay rise that you want.

Netflix is recognised as one of the best companies in the world to work for. Their culture is unique, and they make explicit reference to what we have discussed above in one of their guiding principles around managing their people's pay.

'Pay Top of Market is core to high performance culture. One outstanding employee gets more done and costs less than two adequate employees. We endeavour to only have outstanding employees'.

Think about how you are acting and behaving at work, does it reflect the work done by someone who deserves more pay?

Just as a final point, always try and look at these conversations with your boss from their perspective. Blackmail of any sort, be it emotional or through gathering offers from other companies, will leave a sour taste in the mouth. If you intend to stay at the organisation, then these methods will not make you popular within the business over the long term.

Ultimately, whether you like it or not, you will find that if you don't ask you won't get so I would encourage you to be respectful but proactive in making sure you are paid what you are worth.

Passive Income

Monopoly remains one of the world's most popular boardgames with over 250 million sets sold in 103 countries in 37 languages. In the game, players build up housing and hotel empires that generate income with the winner usually being the player who secures the most squares on the board.

Despite being just a game, there are some useful lessons to be learnt regarding how we manage our money and careers. For example, you will never win Monopoly by just trying to pass go and collect £200, but that's what most people do in real life, in other words relying on a single regular income and ignoring opportunities to develop additional revenue streams.

Former Monopoly world champion Bjørn Halvard Knappskog also points out that, 'too many amateurs make the mistake of focusing exclusively on the most expensive streets, sitting on their cash until they get the chance to buy Boardwalk. Never do this, by which I mean never! Attaining a monopoly is much more lucrative than buying expensive property on which you can no longer afford to build. Think small to generate a sustainable cash flow'.

This is great advice from Bjorn, and in the real world, when looking at building additional sources of income, it is often worth starting out small and building things up over time.

Passive income is the holy grail of wealth creation. This is income that is generated without you lifting a finger. This is what true financial freedom looks like where your financial commitments are met whether you decide to get up for work or not.

Typically, we find passive income creation is the area that people are least likely to try and exploit. Looking for additional sources of income is not easy, and many people believe impossible. So why, if passive income is the key to financial freedom, don't more people try and develop it?

The main reason, which will sound familiar, is that we don't have enough time with job, kids, commuting and life always getting in the way. It all goes back to mindset.

I have always liked a quote from the Terminator himself, Arnold Schwarzenegger, who is a true expert at time management and positive mindset:

'I've always figured out that there are 24 hours a day. You sleep for six hours and have 18 hours left. Now, I know there are some of you out there that say well, wait a minute, I sleep eight hours or nine hours. Well, then, sleep faster, I would recommend'.

When Arnold first came to America, he quickly showed that his drive and motivation put him in a different league to anyone else around him. During the day he worked in construction; when his colleagues went home, he would go to the gym for 5 hours. After those he worked out with went home, he would take acting classes from 8:30 pm until midnight. After this, he would go home, sleep 6 hours and repeat.

Arnold did this brutal regime until he got what he wanted, and the rest is history. Many people don't know this, but Arnold was a property millionaire generating thousands in passive income before he became a well-known film star. Before buying a home to live in, Arnold realised he should first buy an income-producing property so he bought a block of six apartments, lived in number 6 and rented the other 5 out.

Look at your daily routine and try and break it down into 24 hours. Increasingly people are spending more time on their smartphones. Most smartphones now have usage features and will tell you how much time you are spending on your phone and in what apps. Check out the results; it might shock you. The average American, according to eMarketer research, is spending almost 4 hours per day on their phone. Think about that. If you could earn just £5 an hour for 4 hours a day, that would be worth £7,300 at the end of one year.

TV and Mobile Devices: Average Time Spent in the US, 2014-2021
hrs:mins per day among population

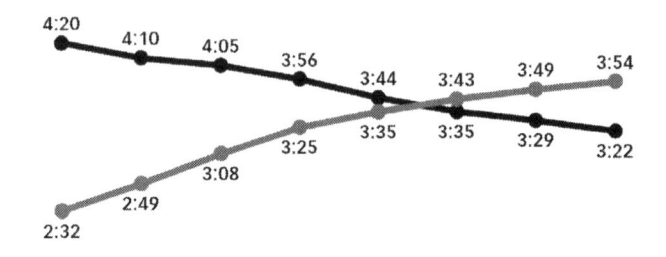

	2014	2015	2016	2017	2018	2019	2020	2021
TV*	4:20	4:10	4:05	3:56	3:44	3:43	3:29	3:22
Mobile devices	2:32	2:49	3:08	3:25	3:35	3:35	3:49	3:54

Note: ages 18+; time spent with each medium includes all time spent with that medium, regardless of multitasking; for example, 1 hour of multitasking on desktop/laptop while watching TV is counted as 1 hour for TV and 1 hour for desktop/laptop; *excludes digital
Source: eMarketer, April 2019

T10195   www.eMarketer.com

What are you spending the most time on? If you are anything like the average person, there will be a lot of wasted time spent browsing your phone or reading 'news'. Social media is not free as many of us believe. It takes your time and usage data and then sells it to advertisers. Their goal is to distract you, and they are very good at it.

Things to Consider When Picking a Passive Income Strategy

Once you have carved out time to work on a passive income side project, before you start, you need to understand a few crucial things.

Pick Something that Interests You

Daniel Grove, a confessed nerd and talented photographer, combined his love of science fiction and photography to offer fun portrait sessions for lovers of 'Star Wars', 'Harry Potter' and other sci-fi favourites. Since gaining momentum within this niche, he has also expanded his service to include more regular work doing wedding and family photography; however, he still specialises in cosplay photography. Daniel's side hustle combines his love of photography with his desire to help people capture special moments. Currently, this side hustle is earning him an average of $1,600 a month on top of his regular day job. You are likely to have to do a large amount of research and work on your chosen topic to be successful, so to keep yourself from going insane, try and pick something that you don't find wildly dull.

It May Take a Little Time to Get Going

Mitch Bowler knew early on that he was not going to be the kind of person who had a normal 9–5 job. He grew up in the tiny village of Manitoba, Canada, which meant few opportunities in what many would call a traditional job.

When he finished art school in 2002, Mitch made the decision to move out to China where he taught English in order to make a living. He quickly realised that to make enough money from this avenue, he would need to teach kids in groups, making it cheaper for them but overall generating more revenue for him. This meant he could cut his workweek down to just 8 hours and look at other opportunities to make money.

Improving his art skills in his spare time meant that Mitch moved jobs and started working at a Chinese studio that supplied art to big video game companies, such as EA and Activision. However seeing an opportunity he began drawing in his spare time and filming the results, turning them into lessons on his website DrawingCoach.com and YouTube. Getting this side hustle going cost him under $100.

Gradually, Mitch saw his income rising as his videos ranked higher on YouTube and advertising revenue increased. In the early days this was only around $30 per month; however, after 5 years spent building up his profile, Mitch had enough money being generated by this source to quit his job.

Expect that initially, it will take some time to set up passive income streams before it reaches escape velocity and can be managed with little or no interference. Remember, if it was easy, everyone would be doing it, so expect to have to jump many hurdles to get it going. Often, the ideas where 99% of people gave up before they got the idea running, or those with high barriers to entry will likely be the longest lasting money spinners.

Be Prepared to Fail

Don't be afraid to give multiple ideas a try and quickly ditch those that don't have much potential. In Mitch's case, he now has three different side hustles running at the same time to try and reduce the risk of his earnings drying up in any one business. There is no hard and fast way to say which ideas will be good and which bad as it all depends on timing and market conditions so make sure you stay diversified in your ideas.

Due to this high failure rate, you must ensure that testing out an idea is not going to break the bank as this can make failure painful and prohibit you from doing future experiments. Mitch spent under $100 setting up his first business with just a camera tripod and a few materials. How much you can afford to spend on each idea depends on your circumstances. If you have very little money, you may want to keep these experiments to under £100, so it won't financially cripple you if it fails. If you are already very rich, then you can commit much more to testing these ventures.

How to Execute Your Side Hustle

To get your side hustle going, you're going to need a solid plan of action. You are also going to need to validate any idea you have.

Remember, this is a side hustle and your first attempts are likely to fail so don't go quitting your job just yet. What we want is validation from an impartial audience that the product or service that we are going to provide does have solid demand out there in the market. For this reason, we want to build a Minimum Viable Product (MVP).

MVP

Eric Ries in his must-read book, 'The Lean Start-Up', talks about what an MVP should achieve. A core component of the Lean Start-Up methodology is the build-measure-learn feedback loop. The first step is figuring out the problem that needs to be solved and then developing an MVP to begin the process of learning as quickly as possible. Once the MVP is established, a start-up can work on tuning the engine. This will involve measurement of key metrics such as user satisfaction and willingness to recommend, sometimes called the net promoter score, and then going back and improving the product for a relaunch.

Your MVP should provide feedback and data from real users as quickly as possible, and this should then be incorporated into the next iteration of your product to ensure it rapidly improves. The speed or velocity in which you receive feedback, improve the product and retest it will be fundamental to the success of your project.

Let's take an example of what not to do.

Before the iPhone, there was the BlackBerry, or 'CrackBerry', as the devices' obsessed users affectionately referred to them. Nothing showed a dedication to your job and companies' mission like hammering away on your blackberry at all times of the day and night. For many, they were the first introduction to owning a smartphone and the first time we connected to the internet using a mobile device. Amongst other innovations, it also seamlessly sent and received email, and gave us access to chat with anyone using the company's BlackBerry Messenger. The Blackberry was immensely successful even when smartphone adoption was relatively low, and they sold more than 50 million devices in 2011.

Blackberry should have been the frontrunner in the smartphone market as it was ideally placed to leverage its position and brand recognition to iterate its product as better processors, screens and third-party apps changed the way we interact with our phones. However, like other slow-moving behemoths, it chose instead to go the way of Nokia's phone division which, at its peak was worth £300 billion, however was eventually broken up and sold for £350 million.

Blackberry simply failed to keep up with the times and its product approach was incredibly stubborn. Their belief that their trademark clunky keyboard was how people wanted to type into their phones, and this made them miss the tectonic shift of user preferences to full touchscreen, which was not only more convenient but quickly became fashionable. User testing and feedback was ignored, and Blackberry simply didn't respond to market forces despite having the information right in front of them. Apple, Samsung and Android quickly eroded their market position, and by 2016, BlackBerry was selling only about 4 million devices annually (a 92% reduction from their peak sales).

BlackBerry still exists today, but as the chart below shows, it is a shadow of its former self despite being the leader in what would become a trillion-dollar market.

Blackberry Revenues 2004–2018 (Source: Statista)

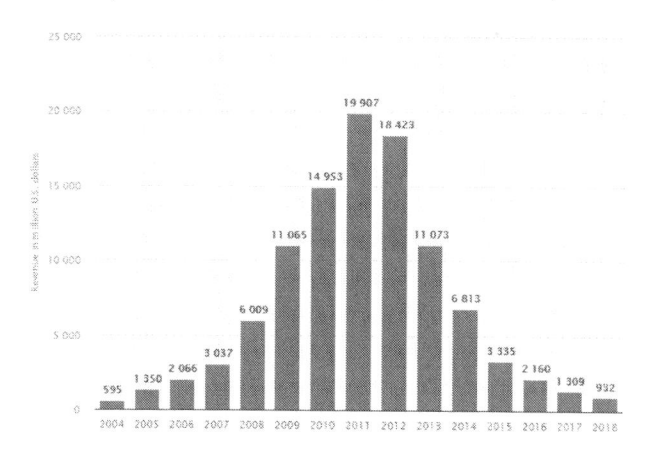

Year	Revenue (millions U.S. dollars)
2004	595
2005	1 350
2006	2 066
2007	3 037
2008	6 009
2009	11 065
2010	14 953
2011	19 907
2012	18 423
2013	11 073
2014	6 813
2015	3 335
2016	2 160
2017	1 309
2018	932

So, what can we learn from Blackberry?

1. Remain flexible and don't be afraid to challenge your thinking.
2. Get feedback quickly and from multiple sources, iterate and re-release. Spin that product flywheel!
3. Keep an eye on shifting consumer preferences; they may hold the key to why your product or service isn't selling or why sales are declining.

Luckily, you don't need the vast resources of Blackberry or Nokia to follow the three points above; remaining flexible is just about having an open mindset. Getting feedback has never been easier, thanks to the multiple review sites and other feedback opportunities, and monitoring consumer trends is easily done with social media.

Finding the Right Side Hustle

We have spoken already about how to link a side hustle with a day job. However, for any number of reasons, this might not be feasible. Perhaps you are doing a job you hate, and anything that means interacting further with it makes you feel a little sick!

The ideal side hustle combines a skill that you possess with an activity you enjoy. You should also consider your personality type as this may point you to certain types of side hustle. If you are a process-driven, tech-savvy type, then an online business with little face-to-face human interaction may be for you. If you are an extravert who loves nothing more than getting in front of the camera or a group of people, then you might consider a coaching or webinar side hustle. The message here is not to create a rod for your own back. Start with the end in mind and try and create something you know you will enjoy if it takes off. This will get you through the inevitable setbacks on the way there.

The below steps should be taken even if you are planning on doing something that is related to your day job. You may even find that when you dig under the surface, you are better off doing something that doesn't relate to your work and indulges another one of your passions. Either way, it is worth putting in the research early on, so you are not kicking yourself later when you are stuck filling out people's tax returns on the side for $10 per hour and hating life.

Step 1: What Are Your Hobbies, Interests, Talents and Skills?

This is a brainstorming exercise. Take time to think about what you enjoy. One question that expert side hustlers ask themselves is, 'what kind of activity makes me completely lose track of time?' When we lose track of time, we can find that we are in a 'flow' state.

According to psychologist Mihály Csíkszentmihályi, your 'flow state' is defined as an 'optimal state of consciousness where we feel our best and perform our best'. Mihaly popularised the term throughout his 20 years studying the topic and in his book, Flow: The Psychology of Happiness. Flow involves 'being completely involved in an activity for its own sake. The ego falls away. Time flies. Every action, movement, and thought follows inevitably from the previous one'.

These activities will be completely personal to you. Perhaps it is immersing yourself in coding, playing music and exercising; it could be anything. The idea is to try and pick activities that allow us to remain in this state for as long as possible.

Another test is to consider how proud you would be of your side hustle if you were talking about it in a social situation. It's always more interesting for people to hear what you have been creating rather than what you have been consuming. Rather than discussing the latest thing you bought or watched on Netflix, why not change the conversation to talk about your potential side hustle and see what reaction you get and how it makes you feel.

This first step is crucial as it forms the platform for your future business, so don't skip this key step and don't hold back.

Step 2: Connect the Dots and Look for Trends

Hopefully, after Step 1 you have a big list of activities that you enjoy doing. It is now time to start connecting the dots.

Daniel Grove was passionate about photography and Star Wars. As weird as the niche sounds, it worked for him as he combined the two to form his business.

This step takes work, but you should begin to see things that come together.

I undertook this exercise in 2016 and linked my day job, which often meant walking around London going to see clients, with an interest in men's fashion and a desire to learn about e-commerce.

With this in mind I launched an Instagram page that focused on selling men's fashion accessories. The content I generated was free as I would simply approach people in the street who were dressed well and asked to take their photo for my page. This provided great material and organically grew the page as people told their friends about some strange person who stopped them in the street and put them on their Insta-page. I also found that those I included on the page would then send me follow up photos that they wanted to show off.

One thing I learnt from this exercise is that if you are starting a side hustle, you are still going to have to do your full-time job, so I will stress, you need to be passionate about the product or service you are looking to launch. After a long day in the office at your normal job, you need to have the staying power to then get straight back to work again when you get home. To succeed you need to be dedicated, excited and unceasing in your motivation to make your idea work.

Step 3: Test the Market

The next step that you need to take is a mixture of market validation and creating your MVP. In Steps 1 and 2 you will have come up with an idea. It's now time to start shaping that idea. Val Geisler of email marketing firm Convert kit suggests writing a list of 10 people you know, or can easily find, who would benefit from your product or service. You need to then ask them three questions:

1. What's your biggest frustration when dealing with [insert topic/product]?

2. What websites, blogs or forums do you visit now to learn about or buy [the topic/product]?

3. I'm launching a new service/product. I'd love for you to be one of my beta readers/testers. Interested?

If you can't think of 10 people, then you may not be on to a winner and may need to revisit Step 1 and try and identify something with a larger addressable market.

If you contact these 10 people and discover a way to scratch an itch that they have had for some time, then you have made a great start. By answering these questions, you will have a better idea of exactly what your product or service should look like, have some great ideas for content as you begin to scale your idea and you will also have your first 10 ambassadors for your product.

Step 4: Create Social Media and Website Content

You may be a little surprised now when I say you don't need a completed product or service before you start your business.

If you have reached Step 4, you have already done some excellent work by finding something you are passionate about and getting 10 people interested in it. We still don't know whether people will be willing to pay you for this product or service. That is what we will continue to test as we build an online following.

To kick start your side hustle, you need to start building a social media presence. Which platforms you use will depend upon your product or service with different channels popular with different demographics. For example, if you are looking to launch a business consultancy service, you would be more likely to focus on Twitter and LinkedIn, and if you were looking at products aimed at late teens early 20's, you might consider Tik Tok, Snapchat and Instagram.

Getting good at building social media accounts is something that is worth investing time into. Get researching, do free courses on educational sites like edX, Coursera or Udacity and observe (and learn from) others who you are clearly good at social media. What you are trying to achieve with social media is to produce a valuable stream of content that promotes you as an influencer or thought leader in your realm of expertise. You should not be continually pushing products but offering useful content that creates value. You need to build trust with your audience and then let them come to you when they have a problem that your side hustle solves.

Managing several social media channels at any one time can be very time consuming, and at this stage, this is something that we want to avoid. A service like Hootsuite can be useful to merge your various accounts into one place and let you interact with them in one easy to use interface. It also allows you to prepare multiple posts and then automate when they go out. This can be a big time saver and ensures you don't miss posting when busy with your day job as it ticks along in the background.

My 2016 menswear project built a following of over 10,000 engaged followers by posting original content of well-dressed men around London. The account was there to inspire others who were looking to accessorise their formal wear and helped us build a platform as an influencer within this space. The posts were all automated across Instagram and Facebook and used well-researched hashtags that would generate the right sort of traffic required to build a valuable audience.

To make the most of the traffic that you are generating from your social media profiles, you need a professional working website that is capable of catching people's details. Building a website does not need to be expensive or time-consuming. There are dozens of free resources out there that can help you build one, and it should take no longer than 24 hours. GoDaddy, Squarespace, Wix and Shopify all have incredibly simple website templates that you can modify and can release a stunning website in a matter of hours. They also have great plugins that you can use to start converting traffic into paying customers.

I am not going to go into nuanced detail around exactly what you should put onto your website. There are vast stores of 'how-to' guides out there on the internet, and the companies above who specialise in website creation have thousands of hours of content for the budding side hustler.

What I would like to focus on is the strategy that you are trying to achieve. What you want from your website is people to further validate your idea. For example, for my men's fashion accessories website, which I called Crossbones, I created a website that only had one page. This page looked professional, said a little about why we were doing what we were doing and asked people to sign up if they were interested in buying a limited-edition pocket square once we had finished manufacturing. The site took a couple of hours to complete, and we generated over 300 email signups within the first week with no paid traffic. This might not sound like a lot; however, the exercise was to validate that this was indeed a product that people indicated they would buy.

The same steps could have been used for a service. Create valuable content that supports the service you are looking to launch. Generate traffic via social media to your website and get people to sign up to your free or discounted webinar/book/skype session/conference/etc. You then have a clear measure of how valuable your service is.

Step 5

Once you have a meaningful number of people who have signed up, it is important to not lose track of them. Ongoing email content and countdowns to when you are going to fulfil their request are important to keep momentum with your customers. At the same time, in the background, now you have validated that your idea has legs, you should go about building your MVP.

For example, if you were launching a series of paid webinars, this tends to be simple. Don't go buying a load of expensive equipment; keep it agile and basic. There are plenty of free resources like Skype to carry out webinars, and the microphone on your headphones will probably do for now.

For products, this is more difficult. If you are manufacturing something from scratch, there will always be a minimum order amount which can mean massive initial upfront costs which you may not want to risk at this stage. A better strategy is to white label existing products. Look for low-cost, high-quality goods on sites like Alibaba and order only what you need. Improve and repackage these products and send them to your customers. As you begin to scale, you may want to consider the concept of drop shipping or using third-party fulfilment centres. These products can be sold quickly and cheaply from your own website or on third party e-commerce platforms such as Amazon, eBay and Etsy.

As we have said before, the idea is to get your side hustle into the hands of the end users as quickly as possible and then get their feedback, so you can rapidly iterate and improve what you are providing. This is the quickest way to succeed, and product velocity will keep driving people towards your side hustle.

This has been a bit of a whistle-stop tour of how to kick your side hustle off. It is intentionally simplistic and there are many different routes you can take; you can go online and lose yourself in researching your next step for years. The key is to try something. Even if it fails, as my menswear brand did (more on this later), the real value in the early stages is what you learn from the experience so the next time you get that little bit further. That's why we use the MVP model and launch ideas quickly, gain feedback and improve. If you are going to fail, make sure you fail quickly and move on with the knowledge gained.

Passive Income Inspiration

Don't Leave Money on the Table

Seth Ollerton has three brothers and two brothers-in-law in medicine. He watched them push through years of medical school whilst being married with children. In an interview with Side Hustle School, he explains how his siblings spent so much time and energy studying to pass the board exams to become doctors, that they had no time to learn anything about business, let alone marketing.

In his day job, Seth was an experience digital marketer and was an expert at running Google AdWords and Facebook Ad campaigns. It was obvious to Seth that medical professionals in his area were missing a huge opportunity by not marketing their services properly. With this in mind, he began approaching ones he knew about their online marketing services.

One orthodontist took Seth up on his offer, and they spent just under $500 in the month of February, mostly towards Facebook ads, offering a $400 off coupon for braces. The campaign brought in 13 new patients, with each spending $5,000 for braces, bringing in $65,000 in new revenue, minus overhead and other expenses.

Seth's start-up costs were minimal: $99/month for his website and $69/month for Adobe Creative Cloud for graphic design and video editing. After the free trial, he charges $800 to $1000/month for his services, which don't include the ad spend on Google AdWords or Facebook Advertising. His business is growing but his first two paying clients bring in an additional $1,800/month on top of his day job. Seth's story is interesting as it not only shows that you might be leaving money on the table in your current job as these medical professionals were but that there might also be a quick and easy way to leverage the skills you do have to help those around you who aren't exploiting their own niches.

Take a look at your current job. There is almost always something else that you can be doing to generate money on the side with very little effort.

Income that is closely aligned with your day job is often referred to as continuity income. For example, building on Seth's story, if you're a dentist, you are probably seeing patients once or twice a year where they will pay you a fee. This is where most dentists would stop. A great way to build a passive income with these patients would be to sell them a subscription to a service which might whiten their teeth as well as ensuring when you do have them in the office that they are stocking up with toothpaste and the latest brushes.

Another profession where the ability to upsell and build passive income is obvious is for personal trainers. The average personal trainer would meet with clients a few days a week and collect their money, but this is leaving serious cash on the table. If you are spending a lot of time in the gym advising clients, it makes sense to record some of your training tips and case study clients and build a digital content library that you can sell later. These how-to guides can be extremely popular on YouTube where you can build income via advertising revenue or can be turned into an online subscription service which can be sold as a package and built into passive income over time.

As a personal trainer, you may also be advising on diet and can create a passive income stream by selling clients supplements such as protein powder and vitamins which not only generates additional income but could help your clients hit their goals. You could also look at the many food delivery services that offer affiliate programs whereby simply by introducing clients to their service you can receive a share of revenue with no additional effort required.

I have a friend who works for one of the world's largest drinks companies and supplies many of the top hotels in

London with brand name spirits. This role is largely focused on building relationships with the bar staff at these hotels so that he can keep track of what is selling well and what isn't and how consumer trends are evolving so he can stay one step ahead of the hotel's demands.

It was during these many trips onsite with his customers that he found that bar staff were frequently complaining that they could not find interesting glasses for their high-priced cocktails. The theatre and spectacle that goes with the mixing of these cocktails are just as important as the actual drink itself. Customers also reported that if a cocktail was delivered memorably and tasted great, they were more likely to revisit the bar that served it.

My friend has always had an entrepreneurial streak and quickly saw that there was a gap in the market so he got researching. It didn't take him long to see that there was no shortage of interesting glasses that he could purchase inexpensively online. The issue seemed that no one was targeting the wholesale market of bars and hotels.

With this information in mind, he put together a professional brochure of the types of glasses that he could easily source online which he could then show to prospects. He then made sure that after each discussion with a hotel, he also spent a few minutes showing them the pitch deck that he had created.

After just a few months, he was not only selling new glasses to his customers but also receiving repeat orders as customers stole or damaged the ones that he initially sold. This has added a large additional stream of income to his otherwise ordinary day job.

These examples seem easy as they involve a lot of direct contact with people and the roles described tend to either be self-employed or in niche business areas. But what strategies could the average salaried employee use?

Teach Your Expertise

In any job that you are currently doing, it is likely that other less-experienced people in your industry are looking for advice from experts who have already been successful in their field.

An easy example is sales. Regardless of the area of sales that you are working in, your insights into how to close deals can be invaluable. Much like the example of the personal trainer, are you writing down the hints and useful tips you are picking up every day when you interact with customers and close deals? Could you turn this into a book, podcast or YouTube channel?

Although not strictly passive income, over time as you build up a reputation as a subject matter expert in this field, you may find that you can run workshops and seminars outside of working hours or even get invited and paid to do keynote speaking slots at events. All of the sales gurus out there who are reaping the rewards from book sales and various other sources will all have started from nothing and through hard work will have built their personal brand. Don't be afraid to put yourself out there; the content you create won't be perfect to begin with, but this is an area where it really makes sense to learn on the job.

For those in trade jobs such as electricians, painters and plumbers, there is still room in the market to produce how-to videos that people will find genuinely interesting.

Not only can these videos be turned into useful guides that could be sold or again generate advertising revenue on YouTube, but they will create that virtuous circle where people may even contact you for additional work.

Also, if you build up any following in a specific field, you will find that people will contact you for product recommendations. This can be another source of income as you contact product suppliers and offer them access to your network and take a share of the revenue of any products sold.

It doesn't matter what job you are working in; there are always examples of other sources of income that can be generated from leveraging the skills you have developed in your career.

Accountancy might not sound like the most entrepreneurial career, but there are examples where you can easily find additional streams of income.

A contact who I met through work was working as an accountant for one of the larger auditing firms. He was often asked by people he met who worked at small companies if he could help with their budgeting, tax and operations. Whenever he took these opportunities to his company, he was consistently told that they were too small and fell beneath the level of what was cost-effective – the fees of his company were far higher than would be affordable by the smaller enterprises that were coming to him.

As someone who was looking for additional sources of income and wanted an entrepreneurial side project, he quickly realised there was an opportunity for him. Unfortunately, working for one of the big accountancy firms, he realised that he had very little free time that he could dedicate to do more of what he was already doing.

It was for this reason that he started to research outsourced bookkeeping and found an Indian firm that came highly recommended who helped small businesses with their day-to-day bookkeeping. He contacted them and, after conducting his due diligence and reference checks, set up a commercial arrangement where smaller firms would give him the work, and he would outsource it to the team in India.

As the middleman in the operation, he took a healthy margin whilst still delivering a considerable saving to the small firms who were receiving the service. All he had to do was check and sign off the work that was being carried out, keep the customers happy and when he wanted to, search for more business. This took him less than 5 hours per week, and after a year of setting up his business, he was earning more than his day job with the large accountancy firm.

These are all opportunities and models that relate to the day jobs we are already doing and fall into roughly three categories:

- Outsourcing – is the market you work in inefficient enough that someone is doing your job for less elsewhere and you could be the middle man?
- Bolt-ons – does the product or service you provide benefit from the addition of another product or service? If so, can you cross-sell during your normal working day?

- Adding digital channels – can you leverage what you are doing by capturing your expertise either in video or in a document that can be distributed online?

These will all take time to develop but don't cost anything and once in place can start to pay dividends.

Every Day I'm Hustlin'

Christine Moore had just given birth to her third child in three and a half years. Exhausted and, in her words, feeling 'frumpy and lumpy', she decided to up her training and get into shape for a bikini shoot she had planned. To do this, alongside a strict training schedule, she adopted a strict, low-sugar diet.

Christine was determined to succeed and over the coming months made great progress; however, her sweet tooth meant that although her body improved, it was mental torture. Christine found she would get into a cycle of falling off the wagon and eating sugary foods like donuts and then feel bad about it and work out extra-hard to compensate. This wasn't a sustainable solution and Christine realised she needed to do something to satisfy her cravings but remain healthy.

Christine ordered some whey protein powder and other ingredients she knew fit her diet plan such as flax seeds, cashew milk, apple sauce and the low-calorie sweetener stevia. Out of curiosity, she blended up the ingredients, threw them in the microwave for a couple of minutes and then took out the bowl.

What came out of the microwave was a revelation: a cake! Even better, when she calculated the nutritional content of what she made, she found that it contained 26 g of protein, 2 g of sugar and 16 g of carbs which complemented her diet plan.

Sharing her creations with her friends, Christine received a great response and was soon baking and delivering her cakes for $5 each in her spare time. Her side hustle was called Lil Buff Bakery and has since pivoted to selling her cake mix and not the precooked cake. This has saved on time and shipping costs. In January 2017, Lil Buff Bakery sold almost $30,000 and sales have doubled year after year.

Every day we should be looking to generate new sources of income that will propel us towards our financial goals. Like Christine, inspiration might come from a hobby or solving your own problem or, as in previous examples, opportunities that you spot at work. People who are worth a lot of money will always have multiple income streams.

Data from Bankrate (https://www.bankrate.com/personal-finance/smart-money/side-hustles-survey/) shows that 28% of millennials, between the ages of 18 and 26, are working on a side hustle. If we check out the number of searches for Side Hustle on Google, we can see that over the last 5 years, there has been a huge increase in interest in this concept.

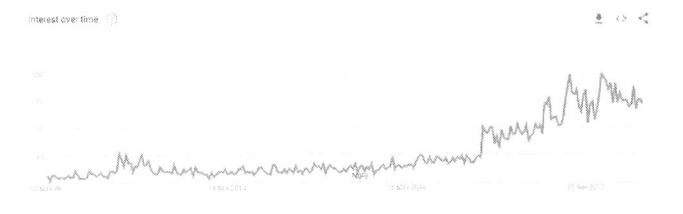

This suggests it isn't only millennials who are often frustrated by their low pay or lack of purpose at work, and everyone seems to be exploring possible entrepreneurial pursuits to find income.

There are lots of great examples of this, such as Nicole Buergers who founded Bee2Bee Honey Collective in 2015 after burning herself out as a corporate marketing executive. She had a mission to provide a healthy, sustainable habitat for pollinators and promote urban beekeeping and honeybee education. Using her skills as a marketer and her passion for beekeeping, she built Houston's only commercial and backyard beekeeping service and online local honey marketplace. She wanted to encourage 'newbee' beekeepers as well as provide online retail services for the established hobbyist beekeeper. This service sounds extremely niche, but through the service and online sales, she nets herself $4,000 per month doing something she loves.

Parker McDonald works as a product manager for an IT company and lives in Tennessee. He has always had an interest in side hustles but found that he had very little time after his demanding day job to put in the effort required to get something off the ground. One day after seeing a blog post that talked about a website called Fiverr, where people can advertise their skills and bid for jobs, a light bulb went off. Parker initially bid and won several jobs proofreading work done by overseas clients but realised that this paid little more than minimum wage. A key leap forward came when one of his overseas clients asked him whether, as a native English speaker, he would do a voice over for a video that he wanted to create. Parker accepted, and the client was happy. So happy in fact that he began to refer his contacts to Parker for additional work. Parker invested $100 in a new microphone and downloaded free audio software for editing, and with that, he was away. Although the sums of money are not huge, Parker makes an additional $8,000 per year, given the time he spends doing it and the enjoyment that he gets out of working with hugely diverse clients; he sees it as well worth his while.

No list of side hustle examples would be complete without some reference to social media. There are thousands of examples of influencers exploring every sort of niche. Given the competition for people's attention in this space, it is not easy to quickly become the next social media superstar and earn millions. However, if you pick an undiscovered niche and produce valuable content, you can find yourself quickly gaining some traction, as these examples show.

The usual social media influencers tend to be models flogging the latest beauty products to adoring teenage fans. Minnesota Millennial Farmer is a little different. He takes us on a fly on the wall journey through his daily routine tackling the life of a farmer. Great videography and honest commentary make for some compelling viewing, and he has amassed 385,000 YouTube subscribers who frequently log in to see what he has been up to. As a fifth generation family farmer from West-Central Minnesota, you wouldn't expect him to achieve any social media fame, but where there is a niche, there is a business. His videos have been viewed millions of times and lead to a large, regular stream of income from advertising. All this from a very simple mission: to help people to trust how their food is grown and raised.

Daniel Gonthier was working as a shop assistant in discount frozen food retailer Iceland. He hated it. Like many people his age, when he wasn't working, he was a dedicated gamer, and this was his real passion. Wanting a creative outlet, he created a YouTube channel in November of 2007 but didn't upload his first video until February 2012. The first video he uploaded wasn't a huge hit as he filmed himself undertaking the Cinnamon Challenge (google it).

Since then, he has taken his passion for gaming and turned it into a hugely profitable business. He specialises in creating comedic gameplay and challenge videos featuring the soccer video game FIFA. He is known as The Gonth, and his channel has earned him 1.7 million subscribers. A native of Wales he has been embraced by YouTube as one of its key influencers and takes home a six-figure salary through advertising and endorsements. The Gonth's appeal is his raucous character and humour, and when not filming new videos, he actively engages with his audience.

The purpose of these stories, I hope, is to inspire you and show that there is no bad idea when it comes to side hustles. If you can find something that you are passionate about and build an audience who engages with or pays for your content, then you are on to a winner. The biggest hurdle to making money from a side hustle is you. I will say that again. The biggest hurdle will be you and the excuses you make as to why it won't work. In the words of Gary Vaynerchuk, 'Ideas are shit, execution is the game.'

Side Hustles You Can Start Tomorrow

It is never too late to start a side hustle. Ross Jackson from Slough in the UK earns up to £600 a month selling hi-fi accessories, on top of his part-time job driving for Sainsbury's (https://www.express.co.uk/finance/personal-finance/938228/Side-hustle-small-businesses-Britons-entrepreneurship-top-up-earnings).

Ross worked as a sales rep in the audio equipment industry for more than 30 years and found himself left with a shed full of stereos, speakers and amplifiers, which he sold on eBay and Gumtree.

His success persuaded him to turn this into a side business: 'I go to auctions of electrical retailers and hi-fi businesses that have gone bust, buy up the stock cheaply and resell it online'. This is a simple business where Ross has combined his love of audio equipment with skills gained in e-commerce to produce a nice little side hustle.

If at this point you are still struggling for inspiration, here are a few ideas that you could start tomorrow. The key, as always, is to keep it lean, test and improve.

E-Commerce

There are a million and one ways to launch an e-commerce business. If we are looking for fast, effective ways to test whether this type of business is for us, then below are a few routes you might want to consider. The benefit of these strategies is that they do not require the creation of products from scratch which can take a long time and cost serious money.

Dropshipping

Dropshippers set up their storefront and process sales, but never touch the actual product. In effect, you act as a middle man. Items are shipped directly to the customer from the manufacturer or wholesaler. Orders are placed on your website and directed straight through to the manufacturer. All you have to do is drive traffic and perfect sales conversion funnels.

Shopify run free online courses which help you to pick products with a high likelihood of success and navigate suppliers to ensure you only buy products from reputable suppliers.

If successful, this side hustle requires little to no money upfront to set up and can quickly grow into a large revenue stream.

Amazon

There are several ways to make money from Amazon, and there are many people out there claiming to be Amazon millionaires. It is probably not surprising to find that over 50% of products sold on Amazon are from third parties. Amazon is a fantastic platform with a lot of motivated buyers to tap into and the fulfilled by Amazon option makes it incredibly simple.

Fulfilled by Amazon or FBA means that all you have to do is send your products to one of Amazon's warehouses and then they will take care of the rest when a customer purchases the item from Amazon.

There are two main ways that you can look to use Amazon:

- Sell your product – look for a niche to exploit. Jungle Scout runs a free in-depth seminar series about how to find a profitable niche and launch a product. I highly recommend their million-dollar case study webinar series to get a grounding in the basics.

- Amazon arbitrage – this is looking for products on other sites or discounted items in shops and reselling them on Amazon. You can use apps such as the Amazon Seller App to scan barcodes and find out how much people are currently purchasing the product for on Amazon and in what quantity. You can quickly work out if there is a profit in a product. Then it is simply a case of sticking an Amazon barcode on the product, filling up a box and shipping them to an Amazon warehouse. If you have done your homework, you can quickly and easily return a profit. This is a simplistic explanation but get googling and learning.

Affiliate Marketing

Where you have built a website or blog with decent traffic, affiliate marketing can be a great way to monetise it. All you need to do is set up the website to refer visitors to buy products from affiliate companies. Every time someone purchases something, you earn a small commission.

Examples of successful affiliate marketing websites are household names such as Moneysupermarket.com, TripAdvisor, PC Magazine and Lastminute.com. These are extreme examples where the sites are making tens of millions a year, but the business model remains the same. Build useful content such as reviews or comparisons, link to suppliers and receive a commission.

Teespring

Teespring is a print-on-demand t-shirt platform. You can custom-design your shirts and sell them through the site. The best thing about the service is there is no money upfront. You design a shirt, create a buzz around it, and if you hit the required number of shirts sold, (usually around 50) they will ship them for you with all profit being yours.

I tried this service after building an Instagram following of over 5,000 people who loved Penguins. I designed a cute Penguin shirt and marketed it to my followers with the added incentive that 10% of profits would be donated to a charity focused on Penguin conservation.

Sadly, I set the minimum order size a little high requiring over 200 shirts to be sold, and with no investment in advertising, the project was doomed to fail. However, the account remains live and interest strong so I can always go down this avenue again.

The Sharing Economy

When creating a side hustle, ideally, we don't want to be swapping our spare time for a simple hourly paycheck. We prefer to create a sustainable business that can work with minimal involvement. That being said, if you are looking to make a quick buck, the sharing economy is making it easier than ever.

Airbnb

If you have extra room in your house, you can earn money renting it out to visitors on Airbnb.com. Not only is it an easy way to make money but you also get the chance to meet interesting people from around the world.

A friend of mine is lucky enough to have a flat near Wimbledon in London. When the famous annual tennis tournament begins, he and his wife will go travelling whilst letting out the flat to tennis enthusiasts. The month or so he can do this covers almost half of his yearly mortgage costs.

If you don't own, don't despair. Increasingly, services are popping up that allow you to sublet your room when you aren't here. You can usually expect to pay a chunk of anything earnt back to the owner of the property, but this is a great way of decreasing the cost of renting. Make sure you check your tenancy agreement and ways to modify it if you are considering this. Also, think creatively about where you might pop up another bed that someone could use in your property. Airbnb was originally founded on air beds so don't think you need to offer a full room to entice a short-term renter.

DogVacay

Currently only in the USA but picture Airbnb for cats and dogs. This platform helps pet owners find sitters, trainers, walkers and even overnight boarders. You can earn up to $1,000 per month, and this has to be the perfect job if you like a furry companion and your work allows pets in the office. There are other apps such as Wag! and Rover too.

Lyft/Uber

Got a car? Well instead of sitting in front of Netflix all night, you might consider jumping in your car and making some money.

If you need any inspiration, Mary England, 28, from Baltimore, drives for Uber and makes $450 a week, working part-time. On an average week, she will drive for 15 hours and enjoys the job 'I find that my blood pressure decreases as soon as I enter city limits. I'm a city girl, what can I say!?' she writes in a message (https://www.thepennyhoarder.com/make-money/how-much-you-make-driving-with-uber/).

This job might not be for everyone, but it is quick and easy to register as a driver, and if you are struggling to save the kind of money needed to hit your financial goals, then it could be a solution.

One thing to consider with this angle is that both companies offer 'Destination Mode'. This allows you to earn money on your regular morning and evening commute by telling the app which direction you're headed and only accepting riders along your route. Monetising your commute can be a great way of getting some extra money going into that saving account each month.

A word of warning, the amount that part-time drivers make can vary widely. Unless driving is something you enjoy, it is unlikely to be the best use of your time as earnings can be low. If however, you are looking for a quick way of making some extra cash on the side to pay down debt or up your savings, this can be an excellent short-term fix.

UberEats/Deliveroo

In the same vein as the Lyft's and Uber's of the world is on-demand food delivery, the same as being a taxi driver just without the people. You can create your hours, drive or cycle around your city, catch up on your favourite podcasts and in the UK, according to data from Indeed.com, earn anywhere between £9.00 and £12.00 per hour. You will need to factor in costs such as petrol, insurance and maintenance into this. It's not going to make you a millionaire overnight but earns you more money than sitting in front of the TV.

Tutoring

Whatever your skill, there is a platform out there which you can use to get students who will pay to learn from you. SayABC allows you to earn up to $21 per hour teaching English to young students in China via video chat. Alternatively, sites like Tutorful allow you to set up a profile where you can talk through your skills and experience, set a price per hour (browsing the site it can be anywhere from £20 to £100 per hour) and then students can search and contact you. All payments are taken through the site and you can either tutor over skype or in person.

If you would like further inspiration on starting a side hustle, I would highly recommend the Podcast by Chris Guillebeau. In his show, Side Hustle School (https://sidehustleschool.com/), he has over 1,000 real world case studies from people who have started businesses.

Summary

How to Earn It is an essential side of the Money Triangle and gives more strength to the other sides of the Triangle. If you earn more, you can invest more and you have more flexibility on spending. Relying on just one stream of income from your day job is risky and can leave you with limited options if you are stuck in a job that you don't enjoy, or feel is going nowhere.

Hopefully, this section has given you the confidence to get out there and at least try to create an additional stream of income. However, it is worth a note of caution. As I stated at the start of this chapter, the easiest way to increase your earnings is to get paid more for what you are currently doing. I would only advise looking at side hustles if you can confidently say you are maximising the earnings you are receiving from your current job. Say, for example, you work in the sales team of an organisation and there are five salespeople. If you are not the top earner, you probably shouldn't be looking at a side hustle. Your lowest hanging fruit is studying why you aren't the highest earner and adopting the same behaviours and strategies of the person that is. Once there is nothing more to get out of your current job, then you should begin looking at other opportunities, whether that be a side hustle or move to a different company if you feel you can't increase your value any further where you are.

Every single one of the people who have built profitable side hustles, negotiated amazing salary increases or just jumped in their car and started driving people about, will have been in the same position as you at some point. The key difference is they went out there and took action. Changing routines and habits can be very difficult, but many of the side hustles in this chapter can be set up in minutes.

The biggest barrier to setting up additional sources of income and increasing the amount you earn each month is you. Yes, the ideas you have in your head might not work, but as long as you can test them without breaking the bank, you should give them a go. As Nelson Mandela said, 'I never lose, I either win or learn'.

Many of the people in the stories in this section went on to say their biggest regret was not starting their side hustle sooner. What's your excuse?

How to Invest It

*'I will tell you how to become rich. Close the doors.
Be fearful when others are greedy.
Be greedy when others are fearful'.
– Warren Buffet*

In 1972, Bob Clark lived in the small town of Bentonville, Arkansas. Although today a larger town of some 50,000 people, back in 1972, it was the embodiment of small-town America. Bob, who was looking for work at the time, found very little opportunity in the town other than working for one of the new up and coming retail stores that had opened, Wal-Mart. Clark started as a truck driver earning near minimum wage which left very little in his budget to do anything other than support his growing family.

However, things changed in his first month when he went along to one of the new driver initiations. At the meeting, Wal-Mart's charismatic founder Sam Walton was there to talk about a new scheme whereby any employee could invest in Wal-Mart and receive a share of future profits. There were only about 15 employees in the room at the time and Walton made the bold claim, 'if you will stay with me for 20 years, I guarantee you'll have $100,000 in profit sharing'.

To Clark, and for most people in 1972, this was an obscene amount of money, more than he could see himself earning in his entire life, let alone during a stint at just one company. Clark recalls being sceptical, but otherwise taken, by the young founder and from that day forward invested in the plan.

Now several decades later, Clark says, 'last time I checked, I had $707,000 in profit sharing, and I see no reason why it won't go up again. I've bought and sold stock over the years, and used it to build on to my home and buy a whole bunch of things'.

A few years earlier in 1968 over in Oklahoma, another employee at Wal-Mart called Georgia Sanders was receiving the same pitch from Sam Walton. Sanders worked as an hourly shop floor worker earning just $1.65 an hour in 1968 which increased to $8.25 when she retired in 1989. Although money was tight, Sanders, believed in the company and made sure she invested all that she could in the profit-sharing plan.

'I took $200,000 in profit sharing when I left, and we invested it pretty wisely, I think. We've done a lot of travelling, bought a new car, and we still have more money than we started with'.

In 1956, aged 22, Ronald Wayen moved to California. He had a passion for electronics and, in 1971, started his first business, a company selling slot machines. Although the company showed early promise, spiralling debt meant that he eventually wound the company up. Rather than going bankrupt and leave his suppliers with bad debt, Ronald chose to spend the next year paying them back which cost him most of his pay. This early experience would prove crucial in shaping Ronald's attitude to risk.

In 1976, Ronald joined one of Silicon Valley's fastest-growing companies, Atari. Known for developing its iconic Pong computer game, Atari had a culture that clung to the free love movement of the 1960s – with the smell of marijuana often wafting up and down the assembly line where the arcade machines were being made. Ronald, then almost in his 40s, was seen as one of the adults in the room and was responsible for building the internal corporate documentation systems at the company.

Despite his relative maturity, he made a good impression on his co-workers and it was here that he met Steve Jobs and Steve Wozniak. The two Steves could often be found debating issues intensely and Ronald helped settle one of these discussions about the design of computers and the future of the industry by inviting them to his home. What followed on that day was Jobs proposing the founding of a computer company led by him and Wozniak. The ownership stake would be 45% to each Steve and 10% to Ronald who would act as a tiebreaker in their decisions. Ronald wrote the initial partnership agreement, and as one of the three founders of Apple Computer on April 1, 1976, he even illustrated the first Apple logo and wrote the first Apple I manual.

Despite Apple almost immediately showing signs of the massive company that it would become, 12 days later, he sold his 10% share of the new company back to Jobs and Wozniak for $800. One year later, he accepted a final $1,500 to forfeit any potential future claims against the newly legally incorporated Apple, totalling $2,300. At the time of writing, his 10% stake would be worth roughly $120 billion today making him one of the richest people on the planet.

Ronald has taken a philosophical view of his decision stating that he believed Apple 'would be successful, but at the same time there would be significant bumps along the way, and I couldn't risk it. I had already had a rather unfortunate business experience before. I was getting too old and those two were whirlwinds. It was like having a tiger by the tail and I couldn't keep up with these guys'.

Apple and Wal-Mart have done phenomenally well as companies. For example, if you had bought 100 shares in Wall-Mart when it went public in 1970, it would have cost you $1,650. That $1,650 investment would today be worth $4.3 million.

Wal-Mart is a standout performer in terms of the return enjoyed by its shareholders, but there are thousands of similar stories where people, through diligent and regular investment, have achieved financial freedom.

How Investing Drives Wealth Creation

How to Invest It is the side of the Money Triangle that helps you turbocharge the money you earn. The money that we invest will be the main driver of when we will achieve financial independence. Ensuring we are getting the best return possible on this money is essential as it can make or break our future financial plans.

Before we kick off, it is worth revisiting just why getting a good return on our money is so important. To work out how close we are to hitting our financial goals helps to revisit the table that we saw in our section 'Who Want to Be a Millionaire?'

Age you started investing	Years to retirement	Yearly return	Monthly investment amount needed to hit £1 million
20	48	6%	324.80
21	47	6%	345.64
22	46	6%	367.90
23	45	6%	391.71
24	44	6%	417.17
25	43	6%	444.43
26	42	6%	473.62
27	41	6%	504.90
28	40	6%	538.46
29	39	6%	574.48
30	38	6%	613.18
31	37	6%	654.79
32	36	6%	699.57
33	35	6%	747.82
34	34	6%	799.87
35	33	6%	856.08

This table shows us how much we need to invest each month to have a pot worth 1 million or more at the normal retirement age of 68. Now, instead of tweaking the amount of money that we must invest each month, let's look at changing the return which we are expecting. In the example we chose before, we used an expected return of 6%. The reason we chose this is it is roughly the expected return that we would get if we invested in the stock market.

However, the majority of people do not invest their money in stocks but instead, choose cash. In the UK today, according to HMRC, the amount held in cash Individual Savings Accounts (ISAs) stands at £270 billion. At the time of writing, the best available return for cash investments is 1.37% per year.

I understand there are many reasons to invest in cash and other low-risk products, but you can bet that most of this money is not being invested in cash for the right reason and is probably sitting in cash investments through a simple lack of understanding. We can see what a damaging impact these cash deposits are having on wealth creation as if this money were to be invested in stocks and shares and achieve a 6% return, it would give UK investors an additional £11.5 billion per year more than they currently get from cash.

Let's look at our table again and see what effect changing to the cash rate of return does on our investment amounts.

Age you started investing	Years to retirement	Yearly return	Monthly investment amount needed to hit £1 million
20	48	1.37%	1238.84
21	47	1.37%	1274.77
22	46	1.37%	1312.31
23	45	1.37%	1351.57
24	44	1.37%	1392.67
25	43	1.37%	1435.75
26	42	1.37%	1480.93

Age you started investing	Years to retirement	Yearly return	Monthly investment amount needed to hit £1 million
27	41	1.37%	1528.38
28	40	1.37%	1578.27
29	39	1.37%	1630.77
30	38	1.37%	1686.11
31	37	1.37%	1744.51
32	36	1.37%	1806.22
33	35	1.37%	1871.53
34	34	1.37%	1940.76
35	33	1.37%	2014.26

A poor investment return means we need to invest multiple times more to get the same result. This is totally unnecessary; all you need is the confidence and knowledge to invest in assets that give you a higher return.

Developing a long-term mindset to your finances is not easy, and it can be extremely frustrating to begin with, but over time, as we detailed in our mindset chapter, managing your money effectively will become less about motivation and more about habit.

A word of caution. Investing in anything that will give you a reasonable return over the cash rate will come with a degree of risk. This means that if you invest your money, you can expect times when the market price will reduce. These periods can last for a long time and feel painful, and it is for this reason that we must be extremely careful as to the time frame of our investments. For example, if you need the money in a few weeks, then sitting in cash is probably the right place for it. However, if the money sitting in your bank account isn't needed and you are happy to tie it up for years, then this is absolutely the time to be looking at other options which should lead to higher overall returns.

Drown Out the Noise

There are thousands of books on investing, all touting new and exciting ways to become an overnight millionaire. These books are, sadly, rarely worth the price of the paper on which they are printed, and their outlandish claims are used to generate sales. We are also in the habit as a society of idolising those that have made money incredibly quickly. It is hard not to be intrigued by overnight success stories. Take the example of Kevin Systrom who founded Instagram in November 2010 and sold it in April 2012, to Facebook for $1 billion, netting Systrom $400 million and his business partner $100 million.

As well as glamorising people who have enjoyed overnight success, the media loves to remind us of those amazing investments which we missed. A recent article by fortune titled 'Bitcoin Regrets: How Much $100 Would Be Worth Today if You Invested Earlier' talked through how if you had bought just $100 of Bitcoin on July 28, 2010, your $100 investment would be worth, at the Bitcoin peak, (you might want to sit down for this) $28,341,266 today. Even if you had waited until December 2013, your $100 would have been worth $2,665. As I write this, Bitcoin has just crashed from a high of $20,000 to $10,000. I couldn't begin to predict where it will be as you read this.

The media drum these success stories into us, making it difficult to focus on the sort of simple investments that on the surface can look very boring, but over the long term can provide an excellent home for our money.

In order to keep your Money Triangle balanced and on the path to financial freedom, you don't need to chase strategies like Bitcoin that carry insanely high risk, but those that balance risk and reward and can be relied upon for long-term capital growth. We want to ensure that even if you don't manage to build that billion dollars start-up, you will still be financially free to pursue whatever it is you want out of life.

This constant stream of outrageous price appreciation in certain investments brainwashes people to believe that you have to take extreme risk to make any impact on your finances. It breeds impatience and a get-rich-quick attitude. I have spoken to people who believe it is not worth saving even small amounts of money each month as it will simply take too long to accumulate anything significant.

I can completely understand the frustration of these people; we live in a society where instant gratification is the norm, taxis at the touch of a button, same-day delivery of goods, why the hell should finance be any different? I want to be rich, and I want it now!

There are hundreds of financial news channels and websites all touting the latest way to make money out of the market. I don't want to overcomplicate things in this book, and I only want to present ideas that anyone, regardless of financial expertise, can pick up. I have therefore used the advice of some of the world's most successful investors such as billionaire Warren Buffet and founder of investment firm Vanguard, John Bogle, to come up with simple steps which anyone can use to invest successfully for the long-term in the stock market. I have then used a panel of experts to provide ideas about how we can avoid many of the pitfalls when investing in property and how to maximise our returns when picking investments in this area.

I have intentionally left out investments like watches, fine wine, art and other less popular items because I don't have expertise in this field. This is not to say they can't provide an excellent return (as well as the benefit of diversification); for example, Sotherby's has calculated that art by underground street artist Banksy has had an average return of 8.5% per year.

However, Melanie Gerlis, author of Art as an Investment, points out that overall, investment-grade art, held for between 5 and 10 years, will give you a return of around 4pc. 'Considerably less than gold, wine and both public and private equity'. For this reason, I would rather stick with shares and property as they are easier for the average investor to find a winner.

Before we kick off, its worth covering a few basic terms.

Property

This remains the simplest investment to understand as we all have experience with property in one way or another. Property has long been the millionaire maker in many countries, with investors able to buy property with minimal deposits, allowing buyers to take on large amounts of debt and in a rising market magnify their returns; this magnification of returns is known as leverage. Increasingly, we are finding that property prices and availability of financing at reasonable rates mean that buying property is no longer viable for most. In the UK, property prices have more than doubled in the last decade, but median wages have moved by only around 5%. You can invest in property either directly or through investment products that track the price of a specific portfolio of houses or even by buying shares in companies that are involved in building and construction of residential and commercial property.

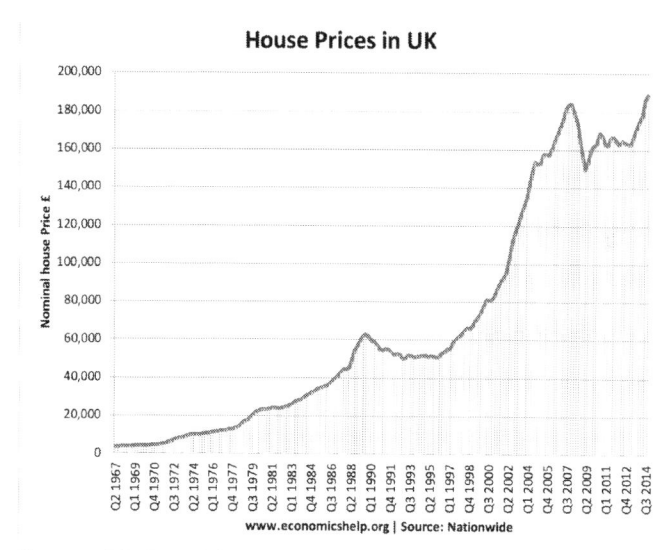

House Prices in UK

Source: Nationwide

Bonds

Think of bonds as an IOU slip from a company or Government. You lend the company money, and in return, they will pay you a regular income. How high that income is will depend on how risky the business you are lending to is deemed to be. For example, if you were lending to the American government, you would receive a low income as the risk of them going bankrupt is very low. At the time of writing, you could expect to receive about 1.83% return on your money if you lent the UK government money for 1 year.

Cash

Cash, as you would imagine, is holding your money in a bank account. Given that UK interest rates were at historic lows following the Financial Crisis, you are unlikely to get more than 0.5% on any money held in cash.

Cash and UK Government bonds are thought of as low risk, and for those who are looking to put money somewhere, they are virtually guaranteed to be able to access it at any time and not see any major appreciation or depreciation of the asset, it can be an excellent place to hold it.

Stocks/Equities/Shares

These all represent the same thing. You are investing money into a company and as such receive a 'share' of the business. Shares can give you a positive or negative return based on the movement of their price and also may pay you a share of profits (known as a dividend) on your investment. How much they pay you is often referred to as the dividend yield. For example, a share that has a 5% dividend yield will pay you £5 per annum for every £100 of shares that you own.

Share Index

An index is a measure of the market value of a group of companies. One you might be familiar with is the Financial Times Stock Exchange (FTSE) 100, which is a measure of the combined price movements of the UK's 100 biggest companies. Others include the S&P 500, which measures the movements of the top 500 companies in the USA and the EuroStoxx 50 which is the top 50 European companies.

The Three Rules of Investing

With these basic concepts covered, we will move on to the first rule of investing that we can draw from our experts.

Rule 1: Make Sure You Take on the Right Amount of Risk

Ray Dalio was born in 1949 in Queens, New York. His father was a jazz musician and his mother was a homemaker. Ray was a curious and independent child and didn't do particularly well at school, finding the teaching style boring and preferring to learn things for himself.

After learning about investing from Wall Street bankers he met as a caddie at his local golf club, he bought his first investment in North East Airlines at the tender age of 12. The reason for his decision to buy this stock was they were the only ones he could find that were trading for less than $5 per share. Fortunately for Ray, he bought at a time that was extremely good for the industry and he tripled his money.

This early success had him hooked and he continued to invest throughout high school; however, he lost almost all of his money in the market downturns of 1967 and 1969. Ray took these lessons to heart and continued to change his investing style to suit the markets.

Today, Ray is one of the most successful hedge fund investors of all time. His firm, Bridgewater Associates, manages

$150 billion of client money, and throughout his investment career, he has built a net worth of around $17.5 billion. What has been most unusual about Dalio's investment career is, with the exception of his early investment career, the consistency of his returns, and this has proven extremely attractive to investors.

Investing is all about managing risk and Ray states, 'I learned that if I could have 10 or 15 uncorrelated bets, and they're all about the same return, that I could cut my risk by 75% or 85%', he added. 'That would mean that I would increase my return to risk ratio by a factor of five through diversification'.

Ray is an example of someone who has a healthy respect for the risk involved in invested his money. Too often we see people setting money aside but with little knowledge of where it is actually being invested. Take your pension, for example; do you know what it is invested in and could you say whether the money you have put in is being invested in the right thing for you?

For this section, I am going to assume that you haven't got bags of money saved up and aren't looking to retire in the next ten years. The strategy that we are using to invest in stocks relies on a long-term time horizon with regular monthly investments over the course of years. The key is consistency. As the pot we invest in begins to build up, we will find that the key to wealth growth will soon be driven more by investment growth and less by the amount we put in. This can be seen in the chart below from J. D Roth's awesome website getrichslowly.org.

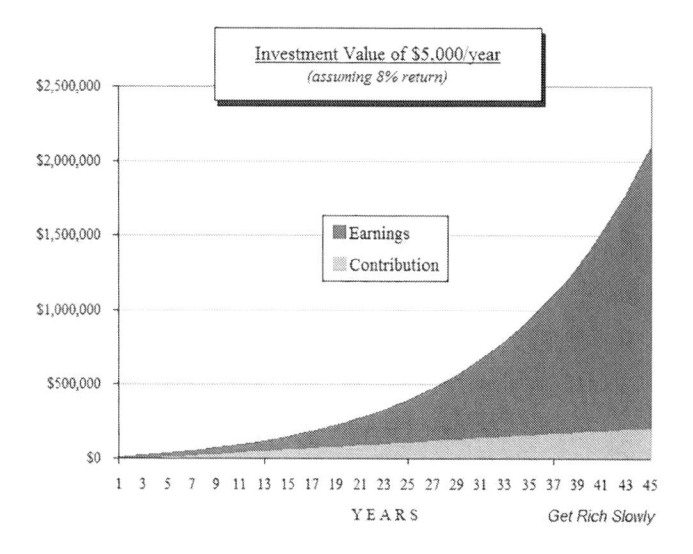

Investment Value of $5,000/year
(assuming 8% return)

As you can see from the chart, in only 7–8 years, the amount of money that you earn from your investment returns is larger than the amount you put in for that year. This is the beauty of compounding and is why Einstein said, 'Compound interest is the eighth wonder of the world. He who understands it earns it ... he who doesn't pays it'.

To improve our chances of achieving the maximum compounding, we must seek out the best investment returns we can.

Comparing Investment Options

'Past performance is not a guide to the future' is something you read in a lot of financial small print. This is certainly true; however, at the same time, we can look at very long statistical trends in the market to see how asset classes compare and try and draw some sensible conclusions.

Over the Very Long-Term How Do Different Asset Classes Compare?

The reason I have chosen to look at these returns over the very long term is that any one asset class can outperform another over the shorter term of say 10 years. As I am looking to invest over a period of 30 years or more, I am looking for trends in outperformance that have persisted for exceptionally long periods of time.

If we had invested $100 in ultra-safe US treasury bonds back in 1928, what would we have today some 90 years later? The answer is $2,015.63 or roughly 20x our initial investment. Sound impressive, right? How does that compare though to other investments?

The Standard and Poor's (S&P) 500 is an index that tracks the returns of the 500 largest companies in the United States. There are some funds that you can invest in that allow you to get exposure to all 500 companies without yourself having to go and purchase and monitor all 500. In other words, it remains an easy investment to manage.

If we had invested the same $100 in 1928 into the S&P500, we would today have $399,885.98, nearly 200 times more than if we had invested in US Government bonds. That is quite a large outperformance compared to those bonds (http://pages.stern.nyu.edu/~adamodar/New_Home_Page/datafile/histretSP.html)

What Are the Risks?

To get high returns, you have to take on a certain amount of risk. There is no way around this. By risk, we mean volatility or price fluctuations which, if you are monitoring your investments regularly, can be very scary!

The S&P500 has had some great returns over the last 90 years, but it has also experienced some significant declines, corrections, bear markets and periods of poor performance.

A correction is when stocks fall 10%. From 1900 through to 2013, there were 123 corrections (about one per year). In the same period, there were also 32 bear markets – when stocks fell by 20% or more (one every 3.5 years), these bear markets resulted in a decline, on average, of 32%.

In the average correction, the market fully recovered its value within around 10 months, and the average bear market lasted 15 months. The most recent bear market, also known as the credit crisis, lasted 17 months, from October 2007 to March 2009, and caused a more than 50% drop in the S&P 500.

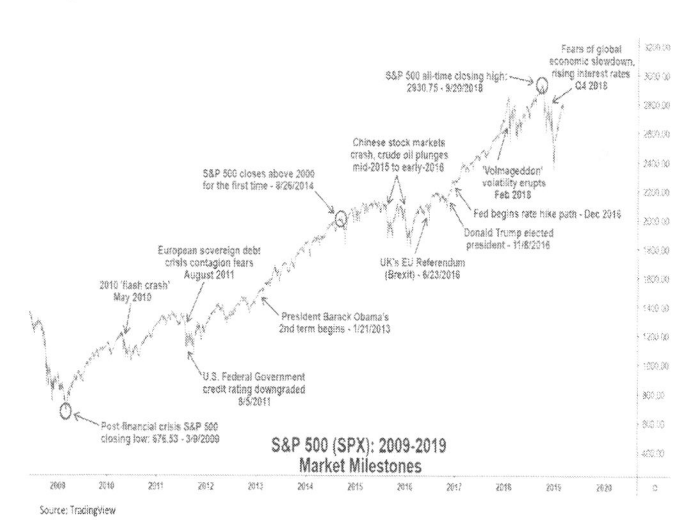

Source: Chris Kacher, MoKa Investors

Human's survival instincts mean we are programmed to avoid risk taking and dislike losses. Studies show that losses are twice as powerful, psychologically, as gains so we feel twice as much impact from losing £100 than from winning £100.

It is for this reason that it is incredibly important that if you are investing in shares, you have a long-term mindset. It is also important that when markets do drop, as indeed they will, that you don't stop those regular monthly investments. During these periods you are buying shares at a discount to what you were buying them at in previous months. If a market recovery does eventually occur, those investments have improved your overall average position.

It is significantly harder to reach financial freedom if our money is not giving us a decent return on investment. There are risks and these must be understood and respected, but we should not be scared of investing assets as we need a good return on our assets to balance this side of our Money Triangle.

As I focus on a long-term approach when investing, I have built a portfolio of investments that invest in global stock markets. I have a monthly direct debit that sends money to my Vanguard account where it automatically purchases an S&P 500 tracker fund and a Global Equity fund. I have always had a slight preference towards US investments, hence why I am not exclusively in the global equity fund. This mix over the past 10 or so years has returned around 9.5% per annum after fees which, with a long-term investment mindset, is giving me exactly what I need to hit my goals.

This is the right investment for me now as I appreciate it may be a couple of decades before I need to access the money that I am saving so I am comfortable taking on a high degree of risk. As I approach the time that I will need access to this money, I will begin to move my money into less risky investments. This will ensure that as I approach the time when I will need the money, I am less at risk of it decreasing wildly in value due to an unforeseen market correction or bear market – this is known as 'lifestyling'.

Rule 2: Don't Try to Beat the Market

Jim Cramer had a long and distinguished career at Wall Street heavyweight Goldman Sachs before becoming the host of Mad Money on CNBC. As part of the show, he gives buy and sell recommendations on specific stocks in his trademark high energy style. Jim is the typical financial news talking head, full of outlandish claims and jumping on the back of any news that might have an impact on stocks.

Jim is considered an 'expert' when it comes to stock selection having spent his entire career on Wall Street. Despite his vast experience, even he is likely to get things wrong:

'We are buying some of every one of these this morning as I give this speech. We buy them every day, particularly if they are down, which, no surprise given what they do, is very rare. And we will keep doing so until this period is over'.

This was Jim on Tech stocks in the year 2000, the month before the index began an 80% decline as the dotcom bubble burst. He also failed to act during the financial crisis in

2007 touting banking stocks during a period when many of them were on the verge of bankruptcy.

A recent study by S&P Dow Jones Indices (https://eu-.spindices.com/documents/spiva/spiva-europe-year-end-2015.pdf) compares the return of the stock market with the return of funds managed on an active basis. By active we mean the manager of the fund will try to time when she is investing in the market and will buy more of certain shares that she thinks will outperform the market. In other words, they are actively managing the investment and trying to beat the return of the underlying index.

Of the 25,000 active funds studied, it was found that in Europe, 80% of active managers, like our friend Jim Cramer, failed to beat the benchmark index over the past 5 years, rising to 86% over the past decade (http://www.technologyinvestor.com/?p=34189).

Warren Buffett, one of the richest men in the world and recognised as one of the greatest stock pickers of the century, had this to say about how the average investor could beat a professional:

'By periodically investing in an index fund, for example, the know-nothing investor can actually outperform most investment professionals. Paradoxically, when 'dumb' money acknowledges its limitations, it ceases to be dumb'.

Investing is a zero-sum game. If you are buying, then someone is selling, so one of you is guaranteed to lose money. Now consider that large institutional investors do most transactions in the market and have decades of experience, millions of dollars of funds behind them and the ability to monitor the market 24 hours a day. How does the lonely person on the street feel they can beat them?

Therefore, when investing our money for the long term, we are going to focus on investments that track the underlying market with the minimum deviation from the underlying index. These sorts of funds are also known as passive investments. In other words, we are going to listen to Mr Buffet and invest in something that tracks lots of different companies and gives us an element of diversification, so if any one company does badly, we hope that this will be offset by another company that does well. Passive funds have the added benefit of automatically removing companies that have decreased in value dramatically and replacing with 'up and coming' companies who share values increase and get incorporated into an index. An example of this would be that FTSE100 stalwart Thomas Cook was removed from FTSE100 passive funds in December 2018 as it approached bankruptcy and up and coming food deliver service Just Eat was added.

For the casual investor, it is also incredibly difficult to time when the right time to buy and sell is. For this reason, I wouldn't suggest you try and pick times when you think the market is cheap or when it is expensive. History, and the underperforming experts, show us it is just too difficult to predict.

As we saw in the last segment, the market will go through regular corrections and bear markets. It is for this reason that we will not try and time our investments but invest our money every month. Sometimes, we will purchase stocks when they are a little expensive, and at others, they will be very cheap. The crucial part is we will invest consistently each month and overall expect to perform in line with the market.

Going back to the investments that I use. The global index fund is a passive investment with the manager only trying to copy the underlying index and not pick winners. The same goes for my S&P 500 tracker where the fund manager is measured on how closely he mirrors the returns of the underlying index. In other words, I am not trying to beat the market but simply copy the returns the index makes, which over the long term should prove a successful strategy.

Rule 3: Keep an Eye on Fees

When you invest in a fund, there will be a charge for the cost of buying stocks, administration, reporting requirements, etc. This is usually called the Annual Management Charge (AMC). If you were to invest £100 in a fund and there was an annual management charge of 1%, you can expect to pay £1 per year. It doesn't sound like a lot (particularly as we are used to seeing much higher percentages in everyday life (eg 25% off), but these fees can really add up.

Let's take an example where you invest in two funds.

1. You put £100 per month into fund A which, over 20 years, returns 6% before fees. The AMC for this fund is 1%.

2. You put £100 per month into fund B which, over 20 years, returns 6% before fees. The AMC for this fund is 0.5%.

In example 1, at the end of the 20-year period, your investment would be worth £41,103.

In example 2, at the end of the 20-year period, your investment would be worth £43,562.

That 0.5% difference per year in charges has ended up costing you £2,459 over the term of your investment. If you had held these investments for 30 years, this goes up dramatically. Your investment with a 1% AMC is worth £83,225 versus £91,361 for the 0.5% AMC or a difference of £8,136!

It begs the question of why anyone would invest in these expensive funds. The answer is often these funds fall into the 'active' category that we discussed before. In other words, you are paying the fund manager more for them to 'beat' the market. As we have seen from the data in the previous example, this only occurs for a very small percentage of these actively managed funds. In other words, you are paying more for worse performance!

It is for these reasons that the funds I have chosen are passive investments that track the performance of the stock market and only cost me between 0.08% and 0.25% per year.

Tax

According to amercianfortaxfairness.org, the richest 1% of Americans own 35% of the nation's wealth. The bottom 80% own just 11%. In America, the top income tax rate is 43.4%; however, due to clever accounting and tax write offs, the top 1% have an average tax rate of just 24.7%.

To reduce your tax rate, you don't necessarily need to pay expensive tax consultants as billionaires do. There are many government-backed tax-efficient savings vehicles that provide incentives to get people saving which will mean you can claim back income tax paid on what you invest and not have to pay any tax on the gains that your investments make.

If we take the UK as an example, the most popular tax-efficient investments are pensions and Individual Savings Accounts (ISAs). With a pension, any money up to a maximum of £40,000 per year (for someone earning the average salary) that you put in will be tax free, so depending on your tax rate you can claim back 40%+. Any investment return within your pension is then tax free. When you retire you can take 25% of your saving pot as a tax-free lump sum. However, anything you take out after this will be subject to normal income tax rules. It is important to understand that you cannot access this money until the age of 55 or 58 from 2028 (at time of writing) without some significant tax penalties.

ISAs are a simple solution whereby any money you put in can grow tax free. There are no limits on when this money can be taken out and you can currently put a maximum of £20,000 per year into an ISA.

This may seem very complicated, but a little effort spent researching tax-efficient investment options can massively reduce the amount of tax you pay and ensure you reach your financial goals faster. For example, investing money into a pension can mean every £60 you put in gets topped up to £100 immediately, plus your employer may match your contribution with another £100. This is a risk-free return that is hard to beat!

Summary on Stock Market Investing

When investing our money for the long term, we are going to:

- Take adequate and appropriate risk and look at shares as long-term investments
- Invest regularly and do not try to time the market
- Not try to beat the market so only invest in passive index trackers
- Pick funds with the lowest annual management charge and least deviation from the index
- Maximise the free money available to you from the government by investing as much as we can in tax-efficient investments such as ISAs and pensions

Property

In 1991 Vicki Wusche was in a desperate situation. She had recently fled a violent relationship with her daughters, 1-year-old Charlie and Kimberley, aged 3, to live with her parents.

The three crammed themselves into a box room before finally managing to move into a council house where they ended up staying for three years.

In an interview with Express newspaper, Vicki describes her daily struggle of counting every penny and searching the discount aisle in budget supermarkets often 'in tears' as she struggled to put food on the table for her children.

Her abusive partner provided no maintenance and Vicki was forced to live on Jobseekers' Allowance, which amounted to only £250 a month for the family of three.

Instead of wallowing in self-pity, Vicki chose to enrol on a university course and further her education.

Vicki, who by this point was 51, and living in Uxbridge, in west London, said, 'I knew I didn't want to be dependent on the state for the rest of my life and I didn't want to cause my parents any more stress'.

Vicki spent the next 3 years working incredibly hard, at one point even having five jobs which she juggled with getting her kids to and from school. Her hard work paid off and in 1995 she graduated with a first-class degree in Business and Computing and landed a job as a lecturer.

Having lived on a tight budget for the past few years, Vicki continued to be frugal and was able to put a 15% deposit down on a property by 2008 which she rented out, but Vicki didn't stop there. She now has 22 properties worth more than £2 million that are rented out all over the country. Understanding the needs of those on benefits, she has stuck with properties that can be rented out to government subsidised families which have led to steady consistent returns on her portfolio. She has also subsidised this rental income by starting a company called The Property Mermaid that trains others how to emulate her success.

The above story makes investing in property seem like a simple solution to making your millions in a short period of time. However, Vicki took a disciplined approach and enjoyed highly favourable market conditions. Despite some huge gains seen in recent years in certain property markets, if you look at property over the long term, there is a very different trend.

Research conducted by London Business school over the past 118 years has shown that in the UK stocks have returned 5.5% per year, whereas property has returned just 1.8% per year which is below the rate of inflation. In other words, invested for the long term, your money would have *lost* value in property! There have been regions such as London where price appreciation over certain periods has been incredible, but picking these regions and timing your investment can be very difficult.

This goes against a lot of common wisdom where getting on the housing ladder has become an obsession with elder folk's reference to investments being 'safe as houses'. I would stress that when done correctly, there can be huge amounts of money to be made when buying undervalued properties and flipping or renting them. I wish to highlight though that nothing is guaranteed.

If we look at the aftershock of the financial crisis in the USA ,house prices fell by more than 36% between 2005 and 2012. If, like many property investors, you had only put down a small deposit such as 10%–20% and then borrowed the rest, your entire investment could have been wiped out and the bank would have been chasing you to deposit more money to cover the deficit. All at a time when any other assets you might have had, that you could sell to cover the debt, would also be in freefall. We should, therefore, be careful when assuming that our money is going to be safe when invested in houses and always be more cautious when leveraged as even small price swings can cause you huge problems.

History is littered with bankrupt property developers. Shane Filan was part of the successful UK boyband Westlife, selling 45 million records, touring the world and playing concerts to sold-out crowds. He used the money that he earned to build up a property empire and borrowed large sums of money to leverage his investments even further. When the band split in 2011, Shane lost much of the income that he was using to pay the large interest charges that he was getting each month. In 2012, Shane had borrowings of £18 million for a property project that aimed to build 90 homes in Ireland. Unfortunately, as the property market cooled and he was left having to sell the new properties for less than they cost to build them, he had no choice but to declare bankruptcy due to the highly leveraged investment.

Risk warnings made, if property is your passion, how then can we make money out of this asset class? What follows is by no means an exhaustive list of ideas but strategies that, given favourable market conditions, have been used by property investors to make money consistently.

This guide is hardly fool proof or risk free, but it incorporates practical tips from the experts. This is more focused on property developers in the UK, and although many are applicable internationally, you should always check for differences in taxes or property laws.

How to Choose What Type of Property to Buy

There is a lot of differing opinion on whether you should buy flats or houses if you are building up a property portfolio. Fundamentally, what we are trying to do with property is buy something for the right price which is in high demand but low supply. This maximises our chances of someone paying more for it than we have.

To make matters more complicated, demand tends to be cyclical and can favour different types of property at any given time. Let's take the current London property market. Up until late 2015, there has been huge price appreciation driven by interest from international property purchasers looking to invest money into high-end London properties. The ultra-high-end was the biggest recipient of these inflows, so properties costing £10 million and above saw some of the most rapid price appreciation. Big investors who need to invest a lot of money will tend to look for these bigger projects as opposed to buying thousands of smaller properties. It is for this reason that we saw this segment of the market appreciate more than the cheaper end. However, as the saying goes, 'a rising tide, lifts all boats' and we saw an impressive run of price increases across all London segments.

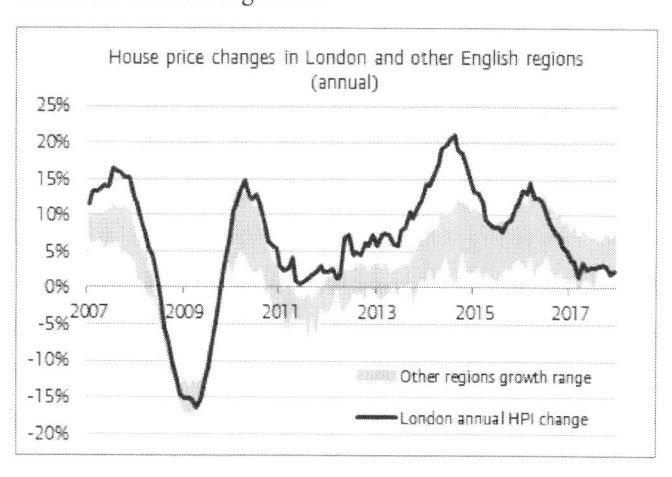

House price changes in London and other English regions (annual)

Fast forward to 2019 and London property has seen some significant declines. The prospect of Brexit has scared off many of the international buyers. Lloyds research showed that in the first half of 2017, the number of homes sold for more than £1 million in London fell by 3,940, or 7% year on year. This has led to the high-end property market dropping by about 20% in terms of prices paid. This could prove to be a great buying opportunity in the long run but currently fear is driving the market, and there is very little movement. I must admit to being surprised by the scale of the property price decline because it has come at the same time as the British pound tumbling in value. This effectively means that British assets are 'on sale' to international investors as they are far cheaper on a currency basis than they were in 2015 and combined with panic selling around Brexit, in my mind, represent good value.

If You Really Want to be a Property Investor

Rapid price appreciation in property prices has left a whole generation of house buyers behind. Millennials are desperate to get on the housing ladder, but there remains a large shortage of affordable housing. A possible solution could be to focus on this segment of the market by investing in undervalued properties that when bought up to standard can be sold as affordable housing or rented to this segment of the market.

Camilla Dell is Managing Partner and founder of Black Brick Property Solutions LLP and has worked in the London property market since 2002 (https://www.black-brick.com/camilla-dell). She agrees that investors who put money into flats tend to generate a good return. 'Generally speaking, flats make better buy-to-let investments than houses, and if your budget will stretch to a two-bedroom, two-bathroom flat, we would always advise that', says Camilla. The second bathroom might sound unnecessary, but the more flexible your buy-to-let property is, the better.

It always makes sense to think about who your prospective buyer is and what their motivations are, so you can best tailor your purchase and any subsequent modification to the property to suit their needs.

With the type of property chosen, it is now about finding one at the right price. This is where the old adage of buy low, sell high is extremely important!

This is the number one reason why people lose money in property. You can pick the best up and coming area with impressive property growth but if you pay above the market price it will take a long time to recoup your initial investment. What you are looking for as you do your research is a bargain. Something that stands out as a no brainer investment that others have missed. To do this, you will often be required to have an information advantage that others don't have, effectively an insight that gives you an edge.

Property is competitive, so when buying, it's not going to be easy to spot a bargain thousands of miles away. To gain an edge, for your first few properties, it makes sense to try and buy something in your local area.

When I bought my first place in London, I knew exactly the type of person I would be renting to as I was living and renting a similar property just 10 doors down the road. My target market was me!

I also knew the potential of the property as I lived in an identical albeit fully refurbished flat and knew what rent could be demanded. I also had detailed knowledge of local amenities being a regular user of the nearby high street and transport links. I had also seen how much investment had gone into the local area and how it had improved with better services for the local population popping up everywhere which hadn't necessarily been reflected in property price increases. All these reasons gave me the confidence to purchase the property as, despite being a novice, I knew more about the local area than anyone buying from a distance.

Having local knowledge is not the only way you can bag yourself a property bargain:

Auctions – by far the riskiest option and require the most homework but can lead to some amazing deals. When a property is sold through a non-traditional route such as an auction, you can assume there is something unusual about it, hence why a normal agent is not used. Make sure to view anything you bid on and read the legal pack. Short or unusual leases are common on auction properties so I will say again. Read the legal pack!!!

Buy directly from banks or lawyers – often you can pick up bargain properties that have come from forced or distressed sales due to bankruptcies or multiple disposals. Banks, lawyers and sometimes accountants, if you build relationships, can point you in the right direction.

Unusual properties – don't be afraid to consider properties that are a little unusual. These include those that might be above a commercial property, in run-down parts of town or even near main roads or train lines. Creative noise reduction techniques, internal or external design can sometimes liberate unseen value. If you can see a market for the property don't be afraid to explore it.

Picking an unfashionable part of town – as property prices move higher in urban centres, we see the huge knock-on impacts for suburbs. Look for unpopular areas with good transport into the town centre, and you could position yourself to pick up assets before they begin to start moving higher. You often find that these areas will have higher rental yields than in town centres.

Transport – spotting when transport links are going to improve in a local area can also be a way of getting ahead of the crowd and pick up a bargain. This can involve studying long-term transport plans and trying to pinpoint the areas that will benefit the most from any new infrastructure improvements. Bear in mind; property is a competitive market so to spot these opportunities before others do you will have to commit time and resources to stay on top of any new developments.

A good example of this strategy in action was with the huge infrastructure project for Crossrail which saw 118km of additional rail network added across London. House prices within a mile radius of any of the forty Crossrail stations that run east to west across London have shot up 66% since 2009, according to research by Hamptons International. That's a premium of 15% more than the London average over the same period (https://www.homesandproperty.co.uk/property-news/buying/new-homes/where-to-buy-along-the-elizabeth-line-the-crossrail-effect-boosts-house-prices-in-southeast-london-a116586.html).

These are just a few of the techniques that you can use to highlight properties that might be on the market for less than they are worth. As always you need to do your homework and check for any obvious problems that would impede future price growth.

Renting Out Your Property

If you are looking to buy property and rent it out, it is essential that you get good tenants. It can be a massive pain at the time to spend extra effort doing background checks, but this can pay dividends later.

A glance at Reddit can give you ample reason as to why bad tenants can cause you some serious problems:

Tenants lived upstairs for three months, didn't pay the third month's rent, called in (as me) to cut off my utilities, reported me to Children's Division for child abuse… moved out leaving 18 bags of garbage & reported me to the fire department for the garbage hazard.
– nachoqueen

I had a tenant pour concrete down the drains. There was no repair possible. It was more cost-effective to demolish, salvage what we could and rebuild. It even got into the septic system, and we had to settle with the city for damaging their infrastructure. Biggest nightmare ever. We sued the former tenants, but when you're suing a scumbag, best-case scenario, you might get a 1990 Toyota Tercel.
– Throwaway1242014

My parent's place, maybe 12 years ago:

They rented out the house to what seemed like a nice family. Both parents, kids, stable job. They paid their rent on time and never caused any issues. After a year or so, my mom wanted to drop by to see how things were going. You need to give notice before an inspection, and we couldn't get them on the phone, so we left a note on the door.

The next day, the guy shows up at our house and hands me a cheque for next month's rent. He told me they were leaving, so long, goodbye. Apparently, they bought a new house in a much nicer neighbourhood. My parents thought this was a little odd, so they went to see the rented house, thinking that there's a lot of damage.

The place was empty and clean. The only sign that anything was wrong was that there were some weird 7⌀ wide circular burns on the carpet downstairs, some steel tubing left against the wall, and a teeny little weed sapling, forgotten in the corner.
– Squifferific

Unless you want budding horticulturalists setting up shop in your new investment property, it makes a sense to do your homework on the person who will be moving in. The website Property Geek gives the following advice:

Some landlords make all referencing checks themselves, but I think it makes sense to use a professional referencing service. (Google 'tenant referencing' and you'll find lots of options.)

For around £20 and within a day or two, the company will obtain:

A check to see if they have any county court judgments (CCJs) against them:

- A bankruptcy and insolvency check
- Any undisclosed previous addresses and any credit linked to their past addresses (because if they're not telling you about a past address, is that because they didn't behave brilliantly there?)
- Confirmation that they're allowed to reside in the UK (although this doesn't remove the requirement for you to do your checks: the Right To Rent law requires that you see the original documents, whereas the referencing provider won't)
- An electoral roll check to see if they can be found at the previous addresses listed
- Verification that the bank account details provided genuinely belong to them
- A reference from their current or previous landlord
- Verification of their employment status and income from their employer

Beware of the Fine Print

Jean-Jacques Rousseau said, 'Patience is bitter, but its fruit is sweet', and this is no truer than in property. It pays to be patient and research everything before you commit to buying anything. Property can be difficult and expensive to sell so bad deals are not easy to unwind.

When I bought my first property, it was during a time when prices were going through the roof with people paying above asking price. Affordable flats in the area I was looking were in very short supply. After six months of looking, I joined about ten other prospective buyers one evening viewing a flat which seemed to tick all the boxes.

It had three bedrooms and one bathroom with access to the loft for a potential extension in the future. Perfect. Or so I thought.

I largely ignored the legal pack in the panic to purchase the property as there were three other offers on the table at the same time and I had to be quick. After some initial haggling I secured the property, and a few months after that initial viewing I moved into the house and began renovation work.

All was going well until I tried to get the windows replaced. Little did I know despite being on a fairly rough looking street in central London I was in fact in a conservation area and as such had to keep wooden framed sash windows. These cost five times the price of modern uPVC windows and required a specialist to install them which took five weeks.

The other issue I failed to notice was that of the difference between a leasehold and freehold property. This does not apply in most countries, but in the UK if you buy a leasehold property you must pay ground rent to the freeholder each year and if the term gets too short (usually your mortgage term plus 50 years) you need to get it extended, and this can be extremely costly.

With my flat, the lease was below 80 years, and I needed to get it extended. I contacted the freeholder and with the help of a friend who was a surveyor I offered him £28,000. You can find estimates for what lease extensions should cost online. Annoyingly, in the early stages of these cases, you must cover not only your legal fees but also all those of the freeholder.

One other point to note is the freeholder is not obliged to accept your figure. If the freeholder is difficult, which sadly in my circumstance was the case, they can contest the offer. My freeholder countered my offer with an amount of £105,000 which was a bit of a shock at the time!

With the guidance of my surveyor, I knew my figure was correct, but to get the freeholder to capitulate, I had to spend an additional £500 with my lawyer to officially summon him to court before we could agree on an amount.

It's important to assess all the pros and cons of an investment before jumping in. In my experience agents will also tell you what you want to hear to get you to buy a property so ensure you do your valuation work before you commit to buying anything. Look for comparable properties in the area and look for reasons why the property you are buying could be worth more or less than what has been paid elsewhere.

Timing a property purchase is very similar to buying stocks and shares. Greed and fear will drive the price of property just as with any asset and as legendary investor Warren Buffet says, 'Be Fearful When Others Are Greedy and Greedy When Others Are Fearful'. When it comes to investing, the crowd is usually wrong, so it pays to zig when everyone else is zagging.

The rookie mistakes I made early on were extremely expensive lessons to learn and ones that if I were looking for a short-term profit would have wiped out anything I could have made on the deal. In property, I cannot stress enough that it pays to read the small print and have extreme attention to detail.

Always Look for Ways to Add Value

Ed Goldswain and Jacquie Hale became the proud owners of No 4 Stanhope Avenue, in London in 2011. They were looking to extend the property by undertaking a cellar conversion which would add a bedroom which was sorely needed as their family was about to grow with the birth of their first child.

Having obtained the planning permission and sign off from the freeholder, they tendered for the work, and five builders applied to do the job.

Talking to the Daily Mail, Jacquie describes how the builder, 'had a good website, and seemed to have been in business for some time. [They] came round to see us, seemed competent and legitimate, and wore a smart shirt with the firm's logo on it'. Happy they had done their homework, they hired the firm and work commenced. Partway through the excavation of the cellar, things started to go very wrong. Large cracks appeared in the flats above which got progressively worse. In the space of a few minutes, the entire house collapsed.

Despite multiple insurance policies, the owners have still not received the money to rebuild the property and now live in rented accommodation hundreds of thousands of pounds out of pocket.

'You read about things like this, and think it couldn't possibly happen to you,' says Jacquie. 'But the thing about this is that it could have happened to anyone' (http://www.dailymail.co.uk/news/article-3015425/Asuburban-nightmare-just-wanted-builder-create-little-extra-space-followed-rules-happened-child-blood.html#ixzz5Et14pde6).

This story acts as a warning that although there are usually many ways to add value to a home, they can also come with a degree of risk. Adding basements or reconfiguring houses into multiple flats can add serious value to a home but require research and planning.

When it comes to adding value to a property, there are hundreds of ways of doing it. Rather than going into exhaustive detail on each one, which may not be relevant to the property you end up purchasing, below is a list of the most common ways to add value and the potential upside to each strategy.

Method	Description	Potential upside
Loft conversion	This will require planning permission and can cost between £20,000 and £60,000. Look for similar projects on nearby properties to see what value was created	22% (Nationwide)
Extra bathroom	Costs of installation can vary wildly from £2,500 to over £10,000 but having a show stopping bathroom or en-suite adds value	9% (Nationwide)
Increase floor area by 10%	This can be done in various ways from converting garages to full extensions. Assume a minimum of £1,500 per m2 of additional space created if you are adding an extension.	5.1% (Nationwide)

Method	Description	Potential upside
Adding a double bedroom	The most successful way of doing this is through reconfiguring existing space. It is often not worth doing if you are losing facilities such as an extra bathroom.	11% (Nationwide)
New kitchen	Kitchens are often the first thing new buyers look at when choosing a home. Current preference is for an open plan kitchen and dining. A new kitchen typically costs £8,000	6% (Which?)
A well-maintained garden	A recent survey that consulted 36 estate agents, garden designers and property professionals ranked the top features to add to a garden to create value: 1. A decent-sized shed 2. Good quality patio/paving 3. Secure fencing / walls / gates 4. Quality outdoor lighting 5. Decking	20% (Yopa)
Adding more light from a conservatory	A good quality conservatory will cost between £4,000 and £10,000. Beware cheap models that will overheat in summer and be too cold to use in winter.	5% (Nationwide)
Being close to a quality supermarket	Sometimes called the Waitrose effect in the UK. If you can buy a house before a quality supermarket is built nearby prices are very likely to increase.	9.6% (Lloyds Bank)

Overseas Property Investment

In my first job straight out of Uni, I worked as a money broker and helped people get the best rate of exchange for their money when making overseas purchases. This was early 2007, and by far the most common reason people were moving money abroad was to buy investment properties in Spain and Dubai which were experiencing a huge boom at the time. The people we spoke to usually had sold up everything in the UK and were looking for a sunnier climate abroad to enjoy their golden years.

Roll on 2008/2009, and many of these people's retirement dreams were smashed with rogue property developers in Spain leaving incomplete buildings as they went bust through the crisis. A serious crash in property prices in Dubai had a similar effect that is still being felt today. Despite an overall recovery in the world economy since then, many of these properties are worth far less than people paid for them at the height of the boom.

In 2014, I bought a two-bedroom flat in the lovely village of Nyon in Switzerland. My wife and I were living in the area at the time, and we felt it was undervalued and there were some extremely favourable tax treatments for residents who owned property in our Canton.

The ground floor flat had been owned for 15 years by an elderly couple and had a huge garden that wrapped the property. However, what set the property apart was its location. Next door was an excavated Roman amphitheatre and a view of a beautiful castle and directly in front was a view of Lake Geneva and Mont Blanc. The place needed a little modernising but had beautiful floor to ceiling windows that made the most of the view and could be lived in from day one.

My wife and I loved both the area and the flat with the view and the quaint village on our doorstep giving us a year-round holiday feeling.

Two years after purchasing the property, we were both looking to move back to the UK, and I did not want to manage an overseas property rental. If you have ever been at the receiving end of Swiss property managers, you will know why. I, therefore, elected to sell the flat.

Since buying the property, the local market had dropped by about 15%, and a lot of the market activity had completed dried up. Having done some low-cost cosmetic work on the flat's interior as well as improve the garden into a lovely outdoor space, we eventually managed to sell the property for 10% more than we had bought it for despite the slow market. Fortunately, whilst we had transferred money from the UK to fund the purchase of the property, the pound had significantly weakened, so when we transferred the money back to the UK again, we had a significant currency gain as well.

There was a degree of luck as we found a motivated buyer in a tough market however, we did our homework, knew the area and bought it for the right price so gave ourselves a good cushion against the market downturn. This selling price as well as the huge amounts of tax that we saved as owners meant we were able to finance the next property when we moved back to the UK.

This is an example of an overseas property purchase gone well, but it could easily have lost me money in retrospect. The point is that when looking for investment deals, we shouldn't solely focus on our home market but wherever we can find value. This comes with the caveat that we must have some knowledge of the local area and the ability to spot something that locals have potentially overlooked.

Conclusion

Jim Haliburton is a buy-to-let investor who owns over 160 properties in the West Midlands region of the UK talked through his strategy for success in an interview with the Telegraph.

Jim focuses on unloved two- and three-bed terraces which, given the area, only cost £60,000 to £80,000 each. He will initially buy the property in cash either directly from an estate agent or at an auction. He will then spend £20,000-£40,000 converting them into five- or six-bedroom houses. He will often then rent them out room by room and would expect to typically make £280 per month per room. For a six-bed house, that works out as an annual income of £20,000 or almost 20% yield on his initial investment. He then has the choice to either hang onto the property and collect rental income or sell it on as the property could be worth up to £200,000 to another investor with income of that level. What he chooses to do will generally be determined by market conditions. If prices are falling, it makes sense to sell the property. If they are rising, then it makes sense to hang on to it.

Generally, Jim will take out a mortgage against the property, of £140,000, or 70pc of its value. This then frees up money that he can put into his next project. Repeating this process and continually optimising debt levels can lead to a significant build-up of value in a short period.

If we want to make money from property, then we must go into it with a clear plan as Jim does. Jim has his target type of property, two or three beds houses in the West Midlands, a way of creating value, adding bedrooms and then a target customer to either rent or sell it to. Keep this in mind when buying property and it can save you a serious headache and money in the future.

Summary

Ensuring you are investing your money at a decent level of risk and return, whether that be in stocks or property is as important as how much you earn and how much you spend. If this side of the Money Triangle is not in balance with the other sides, your path to financial freedom will be a lot longer than you want.

As we saw from the graph in the book, Get Rich Slowly, the returns you earn on the money you invest, can quickly exceed the monthly amount you are investing. In the case of stock market investing, this is passive income in its purest form and all you have to do is sit back and watch your money grow via the miracle of compound interest.

Many will find the section on investing in the stock market overly simplistic, and this is exactly what I am trying to achieve. For the average investor, the complex strategies described in many investing books will be too difficult, time-consuming or costly to follow. I am happy to stick with the advice of one of the richest men on the planet Warren Buffet and develop a strategy of, 'periodically investing in an index fund.'

Property can be an excellent investment and in some cases there can be valuable tax incentives, however, more research and ongoing work is required to ensure your portfolio performs as you wish than with stocks and shares. The leverage from borrowing money to buy property that magnifies potential returns can be attractive, but this is a double-edged sword and as with financial markets, you can expect periodic downturn to hit the value of your portfolio.

Overall by following many of the lessons of the experts within their respective fields you will avoid many of the pitfalls that amateur investors make when trying to either invest in the stock market or property investments. This is by no means an exhaustive list so I would encourage you always to continue to educate yourselves in this area and…. do your homework!

Your Money Triangle

'Early to bed, early to rise, keeps you healthy, wealthy and wise'.
– Benjamin Franklin

The three elements of the Money Triangle are all essential if you are to reach the point of financial freedom in the time frame that you desire. Each of the three main sections of this book have been aimed at providing hints and tips to help you improve these key areas of your finances.

Where Do I Start?

Hopefully, you have a fairly good idea which elements of your Money Triangle are not where they should be.

If you find you are spending everything you earn just covering essential expenditure, then your priority should be increasing what you earn. That could be by looking at your current job and changing your behaviour to position yourself for a conversation about a pay rise, or it could be deciding that there is little more you can do where you currently are so investing in a course or qualification that will allow you to get a better paying job. It could equally be time to start looking at a side hustle and leveraging your experience to drive additional sources of income.

If you find yourself spending large amounts on non-essentials and getting to the end of the month will little money to invest, it is time to start looking at your spending habits. This might be paying yourself first, so you have direct debits that put money straight into a savings account on payday, thus keeping you poor. It could be just optimising household bills and what you spend by comparing suppliers regularly and ensuring you use available discounts that you can find online. It could be as simple as just slightly reducing what you spend each week on eating out, drinking or smoking.

Finally, if you look at the money you do have invested and see that it could be working harder for you, you need to focus on improving where it is invested. This might be ensuring it is invested in assets such as stocks and shares that give you good growth rates over the long term or invested in property that provides additional income or value increases through adding value to the property before you sell it. You should ensure that the money that is invested isn't somewhere with high fees that eat into your returns and it is invested in a tax efficient wrapper.

Many of the people that I speak to aren't intentionally neglecting any one side of the Money Triangle but will have lots of small inefficiencies that, as per our 1% rule championed by Team Sky, really add up to large negative impacts on their road to financial freedom.

When you have your Money Triangle in balance, you should find the benefits extend well beyond your finances. For example, knowing you are being paid what you are worth and maximising what you earn for the skills you possess, you should feel proud. You are achieving your absolute best with what you have and being rewarded appropriately. You should feel more valued and motivated in all that you do knowing that there is little inefficiency in how you use the talents that you have learnt.

Optimising your spending will allow you to feel confident that you are getting value for the money that you have earnt. You aren't doing anything frivolous and only spending when you feel you have found something of real value to you. Many people who have achieved this have found that they become better at identifying where they are wasting other resources such as time and energy and their whole lives become more meaningful.

If the money you save is invested somewhere that is providing a decent return, you can also be confident that even when things are not going so well in your side hustle or career, your money is working hard for you in the background to compensate. This should give you the confidence to take a few risks be that asking for a big pay rise or starting a side hustle which maybe you wouldn't have had the confidence to do if you didn't have money being generated from your investments.

Overall, by combining these three behaviours, spending, earning and investing, you will, over time, achieve financial freedom. Financial freedom means gaining the power to live as you wish and once achieved you can expect to indulge in whatever passions you choose. That might mean continuing work or it could be only working for a few months a year and indulging a passion for travel the rest of the time. The point is, with a solid plan and a disciplined approach, the choice is yours.

Epilogue

Get Rich or Die Tryin'

There is a scene in the film Fight Club where Tyler Durden holds a gun to the head of a guy working in the convenience store?

Tyler asks the terrified shop assistant, Raymond, what he studied in college. Raymond admits he wanted to become a veterinarian, and Tyler tells him that if in three weeks he isn't well on his way to becoming a veterinarian, he'll find him and kill him.

Raymond agrees and sprints off in terror into the night. Tyler then says, clutching Raymond's driving license:

'Tomorrow will be the most beautiful day of Raymond K. Hessel's life. His breakfast will taste better than any meal you and I have ever tasted'.

You may have gone all the way through this book thinking:

- I don't have the time to do any of this because of my job/baby/commute/sleep.
- The small gains are pathetic, and I need something larger and more immediate.
- I don't have the money or experience to do any of these things.
- I am afraid that I will fail, and people will laugh at my efforts.

Or any number of other reasons and excuses as to why you will not change your behaviour and push towards the financial future that you want.

Here is a simple question:

If I had a gun to your head right now and told you that you had to make £1,000 legally without ruining your life in the next 30 days, what would you do? How would you change your life?

I imagine that all the objections above would fade into insignificance when faced with a potential death sentence. Would you still get up at the same time? Would you hide at work or go and ask for a salary increase? Would you try an online business? Would you get on a bike and deliver some pizzas before or after work? Would you extend your commute and drive for Lyft or Uber? Would you make sure your investments weren't just sitting in cash but were in the right place? Would you more closely monitor your spending and invest any surplus to make sure you were benefitting from compounding?

Alternatively, would you spend hours on social media wasting time stalking random people's profiles? Would you constantly worry about what other people were up to and what they thought about your actions? Would you blame the government, the economy, your parents or anyone else for the tough lot you have been given?

If you had a gun to your head, then it's pretty obvious that you would get a serious move on and get out there and earn that extra money regardless of what others thought. You would work your ass off with every spare minute and pull together every resource you have to make sure you're not getting shot at the end of the thirty days!

Why then does it take the threat of death to get us to change? Why can't we have an inner desire to succeed that is so strong that regardless of whether the gun is there we make the most of every precious moment and use it to push towards our goals?

As you put down this book, there is no gun to your head, no one other than yourself who will hold you accountable if you don't take any action and continue as you always have done. You can toss this book on the pile of self-help books, and no one will say a word.

Brandon Stanton, whose photography has inspired millions, asks, 'Why do so many people seem to love righteous indignation? Because if you can prove you're a victim, all rules are off. You can lash out at people. You don't have to be accountable for anything'. For you to take some of the lessons from this book and go out there and change your financial future, you need to not blame others for where you're currently at or see yourself as a victim. There is only one person and one person alone who has put you in the situation you are in now, and that is you. Accepting this is the key to change.

However good or bad your situation is, by truly accepting that you are the reason for the situation you are in, you can also accept that it is you and you alone who will get you out of it. Accountability is the key to change and will be the driving force behind how you go on to live your life and the success you achieve.

'Never underestimate the power of dreams and the influence of the human spirit. We are all the same in this notion: The potential for greatness lives within each of us'.

–Wilma Rudolph

Acknowledgements

In order to have time to write this book, I can't thank my wife Anna enough. Our precocious son Magnus wasn't even born when I started writing this book, and by the time it was finished, he was an incredibly active 2-year-old. Anna's love and support is a huge part of what gets me out of bed in the morning and picks me up after a tough day. So much of what I do in my life simply wouldn't be possible without her in my life.

I would also like to thank Oliver Payne who tirelessly reviewed some very early versions of this book and provided the foreword. His fair and prompt edits kept my ego intact whilst his support helped me finally finish this project.

I would also like to thank Ros and her amazing eye for detail. She helped not only spot many of the errors in early versions but also helped make sense of much of my ramblings in the early stages of the book.

I would also like to thank the hundreds of employers and employees that I have met over the last 4 years who inspired this book. Their stories of how they manage their finances have been hugely influential and my hope is that this book goes a little way to helping them.

About the Author

Name: Phil Blows

Email: Phil_Blows@hotmail.co.uk

Linkedin: https://www.linkedin.com/in/philipblows/

Phil's 15-year career in finance and tech has seen him use a mixture of market knowledge and leading-edge Artificial Intelligence to help over 10,000 people get their financial priorities in order. Along the way, Phil has developed a tried and tested methodology called the Money Triangle that means anyone, regardless of where they are at now, can achieve financial freedom. Phil used this methodology himself to gain financial freedom in his early 30's and now devotes his time to helping others achieve the same.

With a background in Fintech and Asset Management, Phil's broad experience working with both private investors and global investment banks gives him a unique perspective on the current challenges facing society.

Aware that finance is viewed as complex and boring, Phil is a master of using stories of real-life people to teach how simple behavioural changes can lead to vast increases in wealth. He is also able to draw on his wealth of experience from leading fintech start-ups through to the inner workings of notorious investment scams to highlight useful practices that even finance novices can use.

He lives in Surrey with his wife Anna and one-year-old son Magnus.

Printed in Great Britain
by Amazon